WIN THE CUSTOMER, <u>NOT</u> THE ARGUMENT

by Don Gallegos

Raphel Marketing
118 S. Newton Place
Atlantic City, NJ 08401

WIN THE CUSTOMER,
NOT THE ARGUMENT

Published by Raphel Marketing,
118 S. Newton Place, Atlantic City, NJ 08401

Cover Design and Layout by: The Graphic Design Factory

Manufactured in the United States of America
0-9711542-4-4

Other Raphel Marketing Books Include:
SELLING RULES! *by* Murray Raphel
CROWNING THE CUSTOMER *by* Feargal Quinn
LOYALTY MARKETING: THE SECOND ACT *by* Brian Woolf
THE CASE AGAINST WAL-MART *by* Al Norman
SLAM-DUNKING WAL-MART! *by* Al Norman

For more information on these books and for quantity purchases of
WIN THE CUSTOMER, NOT THE ARGUMENT *please contact:*

Raphel Marketing
118 S. Newton Place
Atlantic City, NJ 08401
Toll-Free: 877-386-5925
Phone: 609-348-6646   Fax: 609-347-2455
Email: neil@raphel.com   Website: www.raphel.com

CONTENTS

DEDICATION:

For my wife Cheri

ACKNOWLEDGEMENTS

I could not have written this book without the help of many people. These include my publicists Sharon and Steve Cooper, who urged me to write this book after hearing one of my talks. Neil Raphel did a marvelous job of editing the book and making it entertaining. Todd Behme did the initial edit of the book and was a big help in getting this manuscript off the ground. There are many people I worked with over the years who provided me with insight as to what good customer service really is, and for that I am grateful. I dedicate this book to my wife, Cheri, whose encouragement helped me finish the book.

PREFACE

Isn't it amazing how many talks, pamphlets, books, seminars and meetings have focused on customer service?

And still, we all get generally lousy service whenever, wherever we shop. Service is so bad we sometimes think that we have received great service when we have actually had a poor experience.

Even "good" service providers are really only the best of a bad lot.

We say, "win the customer," yet we train the employee to "win the argument" with policies and practices that encourage us to just say "no."

We say, "the customer is always right," and then we carefully design the rules and regulations under which our customers are permitted to shop with us.

We talk about service recovery, and then we install voice mail, digital answering machines and voice response systems so we never have to talk to our customers.

We talk about pleasing customers, yet more attention is paid to accounting rules and practices which cause us to feel like we have to prove we're not criminals to shop.

And there's more...

Ever try to trace an un-received rebate?

Ever try to return something without a receipt?

Ever try to get a special product, a special cut of meat, a special service, a certain room in a hotel, a certain seat (or section) on a plane, redeem a mileage program award, change a reservation or even get one?

Ever try to even get a satisfactory response from a complaint?

Service in our service industries is not service, it is expense reduction.

Don Gallegos, in his book, "Win the Customer, Not the Argument," understands this and much more.

Don understands real customer service and knows the difference between good service and the "best of a lousy lot."

He knows and understands the feelings and attitudes of the service givers and talks about service that connects us viscerally with front line employees.

"The customer is not always right." Some customers are jerks, but their dog probably still loves them. And, they're still the customer.

Don is a good friend and has taught me most of what I know about customer service. He was the president of one of the most successful retail grocery chains in America. He rose from buyer to president because of his skills as a businessman and his passion for people and service. You'll love his stories and his advice, and admire his point of view. You'll understand that great service flows from a life view that cares about people.

"Don't miss the trip" and read his book. You'll be glad you did.

Warren Bryant
Chairman, President and CEO
Longs Drug Store

6

INTRODUCTION

My name is Don Gallegos and I'm upset by poor customer service. I'm on a crusade to wipe it out, and I want to enlist you to join me.

This book is about customer service and how to improve it. You'll meet some people in the book that you've met in your business. You'll meet the jerk, the complainer, the whiner, the returner ... annoying people who make your business difficult every day.

But wait a second! When you think about it, the jerks, the complainers, the whiners, the returners – they're not a problem. They are all customers, putting money into your cash registers every day. These customers with an attitude or a complaint are really a golden opportunity to prove that your business can deal with any situation.

The real problem today, the real nightmare, is that most businesses in America do not offer good customer service.

It's so bad that people think even mediocre customer service is something to brag about.

Every day, all of you are receiving bad customer service but you are so used to it, you just accept it.

How sad.

Take Mrs. McNulty. A nice elderly woman, Mrs. McNulty lived in my neighborhood and came to see me during the time when I was president of a supermarket chain.

As Mrs. McNulty entered my home, she raved about

how good our employees were to her at our local store.

She said, "I can't believe what one of your stores did for me last week."

She told me that she went shopping the previous Thursday and when she got home to put her groceries away, she discovered that three items were missing.

"I called your store and the head clerk said, 'Yes, Mrs. McNulty, we found those three items. You can come and get them.'"

She added, "I went to get them, and they just gave them to me – no questions asked, no identification and no receipt – they just gave them to me – wasn't that wonderful?"

My insides started to churn, because this woman, one of our regular customers, thought that what she had just received was great service.

I said, "Mrs. McNulty, what would you have thought if the head clerk had told you over the phone, 'Yes, we found those items. Please give me your address and we'll deliver them to your home.' How would that have made you feel?"

"Oh," she said, "That would have been wonderful."

And that's our policy. Too bad our employee did not follow it.

Mrs. McNulty's perception was that she had received good service. But, in truth, the service which had impressed her so much struck me as pretty mediocre. Our employees did not take the extra steps necessary to really help the customer.

I know and you know that customer service can be better. Much better. I had a long and successful business career and all my success was built around one fundamental concept: improving the quality of customer service.

During my career, I worked in nearly every area of the supermarket industry: buying, merchandising, warehousing and store operations. I went through several layers of management including district manager, vice president of retail operations and senior vice-president.

Eventually I became president of King Soopers in Denver, in charge of 15,000 employees. Every day of my 43-year business career I worked with customers, employees, managers and owners to improve the quality of our customer service.

This is not hard stuff. It is easy. It is common sense.

If customer service is so simple, why doesn't everybody do it? Because to improve customer service, you need a concerted effort from the whole organization. And the attitude must start from the top.

In this book, we'll consider all the people you deal with every day:

1. Customers: We start with the customer because customers are the heart and soul of my business, your business, every business. You'll recognize some annoying customers and complaints, and see what we did in some rough situations.

2. Employees: You have to think of front-line employees as your face to the outside world. Treat your employees well and with respect and that's how they will act toward customers. Employees must be led by word and deed.

3. Managers: Managers must understand the

importance of outstanding customer service and the need to motivate employees to achieve that goal.

4. Owners: It all starts from the top. Your attitude, how you treat managers, employees and customers, will affect how all your employees view customer service.

Once you read this book, you will understand why I think customer service today is so poor. And I hope you will also learn some new ideas for making it better.

Part I
Customers

CHAPTER

1

The Customer is Not Always Right

You've had these customers in your business. You know, the customers you can never please. The ones who want special treatment and are never satisfied with how you do things.

You may call them bellyachers, cranks, curmudgeons, faultfinders, grumps, soreheads, malcontents or troublemakers. My employees call them "jerks" – but guess what: I'm happy to have their business!

I always considered it one of my primary job functions to please the so-called "jerks." To do that, I had to understand what the jerk wants, why all my employees are upset about the jerk and what can be done to make the jerk happy.

Here's a typical situation:

When I was a district manager, a customer wrote a letter to our company president about how unhappy he was with the way he was treated in our pharmacy at the store where he regularly shopped.

The letter was forwarded to me with the words, "Don, please take care of this," inscribed at the top in bold, red ink.

The customer, who all our employees considered a jerk, would phone in his prescription to the pharmacy to renew it every 90 days and then show up twenty minutes after his phone call, demanding that his prescription be ready when he was. The pharmacy was a very busy one, located in a high-volume supermarket.

The pharmacy manager would make "the jerk" get in line with other customers and wait his turn.

The other customers would wait in line as they were supposed to: toe-tapping, rolling from foot to foot, clearing throats, with the hope that their behaviors would move the line faster.

As you all probably realize, no amount of toe-tapping or throat-clearing makes a pharmacy line move faster.

The customer my employees labeled as "the jerk" thought this was very poor customer service. He felt he should not be forced to wait in line like those other "regular" people.

After all, he had been smart enough to call ahead. He felt his call ahead entitled him to special treatment.

So he wrote the letter to the company president which was passed down to me, the district manager.

Once I had received the letter, with the bold, red inscription from the president, I quickly went to the store like a good soldier, asking the pharmacy manager for an explanation of what happened.

He said, "Gallegos, you don't understand. This guy's a jerk."

"Yeah, I know he's a jerk. What did he do?"

"He phones in to renew his prescription every 90 days and then shows up twenty minutes later demanding the prescription… and I've got all these other customers waiting in line ahead of him."

The pharmacy manager blended his description with

hand graphics designed to illustrate his depth of frustration with the situation.

I said, "Well, if you know he does that, then why don't you drop everything and get his order ready for him? Then all you have to do is hand it to him when he comes in."

"Yeah, Gallegos, but what if everybody did that?"

"Does everybody do that?"

"No."

"SO, WHAT'S THE PROBLEM?"

After my brief discussion on customer service with the pharmacy manager, I figured this matter was finished.

Three months passed by. During that time a new pharmacy manager had started at the store.

Soon, a second letter to the president from "the jerk" complaining about the pharmacy service and other problems was forwarded to me, along with the red, bold notation… "Don, I thought this was taken care of."

So did I!

I jumped in my car and drove back to the store as fast as I could to see how quickly I could remedy the situation. After all, I have a large family and I needed to keep my job.

As I entered the store, I stopped by the service desk to visit with an employee whom I knew. I asked her if she knew the customer with the complaints.

She said, "Why, yes. We all know him. He is a real jerk. He causes more trouble in this store."

"Is that right? Does he spend money in here?"

"Oh my, he spends a lot of money in here."

I said under my breath, "And we are trying to get rid of him?"

The employee continued, "My store manager told me if the jerk came in and asked for him to tell the jerk he is out."

Surprised with this revelation, I asked, "The store manager told you that?"

"Yes."

I was a man with a mission. I darted to the office to arrange a meeting with the store manager and the new pharmacy manager. I found out from the store manager that the meat manager also had a problem with this customer. I gathered all 14 of the stores' managers in a room. I asked them what the problem was with this customer.

The meat manager spoke first. "Gallegos, you don't understand. This guy's a jerk."

"I know he's a jerk. What did he do?"

"He came in on a Saturday night and wanted eight steaks, each cut an inch thick, and wanted to come into the cutting room and watch me do it."

"Why didn't you let him?"

"Gee, what if everybody wanted to watch me cut steaks?"

"Does everybody want to watch you cut steaks?"

"No."

"SO, WHAT'S THE PROBLEM?"

The new pharmacy manager related the old problem about the jerk wanting special treatment. After telling the pharmacy manager that's exactly what the customer should get, I launched into a forty-five minute dissertation on customer service. By the end of the meeting, I had convinced my managers that they needed to have a new attitude towards the jerk.

Can you guess the ending to this one?

Perhaps not.

Six weeks later, I received a letter from the jerk.

He said he loves us and thinks our people are great. He thinks the store is terrific.

Here's the point. He's still a jerk, only now, he doesn't think we think so. I looked up the customer's spending pattern.

He spends $9,600 a year with us!

And we were trying to get rid of him?

You see, the customer is not going to change. We have to change or the customer will find another place that "loves him."

The story about the jerk is important not just because it had a happy ending. It is important because how your employees think about customers will impact how your employees deal with a difficult customer.

For years, I tried to infect my employees with the attitude, "The customer is king and we are there to serve him." I repeated ad nauseum the familiar customer service slogan…"The customer is always right."

Whenever I used that slogan, I would watch our employees nod their heads and blink in false agreement. They knew that customers were often difficult, sometimes rude and occasionally dishonest.

The slogan needed a reality revision! I realized this when I saw my employees' eyes glaze and roll to the back of their heads as I repeated the slogan.

So, in the middle of an employee meeting, I decided to revise the slogan to reflect the real world. I announced, "The customer is *not* always right."

You should have seen the employees when they

thought I was about to roll out the same tired bromide they had repeatedly heard. Those glazed-over eyes were replaced with interested expressions as the new slogan became the focal point of our discussion.

I paused, and added to the first part of my original statement, "Customers are *not* always right . . . but they are *always* customers."

"You're right," agreed the group. I then told them to remember another important point: "Wrong customers spend money."

Who cares if the customer is wrong? You still want the customer to spend dollars with you, don't you?

When you impress upon employees that they have to accept customers with all their warts, you are well on the way to instilling a mindset of "My customer, right or wrong." When employees are encouraged to help a customer even if they are sure the customer is wrong, it is likely that the customer and the employee will end up satisfied. The important concept is to convince your employees that the goal is not to show the customer you are right and she is wrong. The goal is to win the customer, *not* the argument.

CHAPTER

2

Don't Punish 99% of Your Customers for the Crimes of a Small Minority

I operate from a simple basic premise: Don't worry too much about people ripping you off and your life will be happier and your business more prosperous.

I recently talked with the manager of the loyalty program at the Hampton Inns hotel chain. They have a 100% guarantee policy which says, "If guests are not completely satisfied with their stay at a Hampton Inn hotel, they are not expected to pay."

Any hotel employee, from the cleaning woman to the bellhop to the front desk clerk to the hotel manager, can enforce the policy. The way it works: You tell any employee you are dissatisfied with anything at the hotel and that employee can give you a free night's stay. No questions asked.

I asked the loyalty program manager if they were worried about being ripped off. He said no. In fact, they have found that well over 99% of their customers are extremely honest. The business they lose from the few people who take advantage of them is far outweighed by the business they gain from advertising their 100% guarantee policy.

Sure, people rip you off. People steal, people lie, people cheat. And you should absolutely put in some protections to keep your business from being victimized.

But don't worry too much about the people who return merchandise . . . or who tell you some fruit they bought was mushy . . . or complain about the late fee on a movie.

Much more often than not, it will turn out the customer had a very legitimate reason to complain. And even if the customer is mistaken about your policies or the quality of your services, forget about it. Just make the customer happy and move on.

The funny thing is, your employees will all be very concerned that you don't get ripped off. They identify with your business and don't want customers to get away with murder. But this caring attitude towards the business will be translated in the customer's mind as a business that treats them with suspicion. People want to shop where they are treated as honored guests. No one wants to be in a business where they are suspected of being a potential thief.

When I was president of King Soopers in Denver, we instituted a "no questions asked" refund policy.

That phrase means just what it says. When a customer comes in to complain about a bad steak purchased the other night...

Give the customer a refund. Period.

We don't want the uneaten steak returned. We don't want the crumpled receipt with peanut butter and jelly on the corner – we only want the customer.

You and I know that this policy can be dangerous.

Employees would say to me, "But Gallegos, we're going to get ripped off."

My answer was simply, "I know we're going to get

ripped off – now that you know I know it quit worrying about it."

They're trying to save me from myself. It's been my experience that, yes, some people will rip you off – but not everybody.

Over the years, we estimated that an average customer was worth $5,000 a year to us. If that customer stays with us for 10 years, that's $50,000. Would you want to lose a $50,000 customer over an $8 refund? The refund is pretty cheap, isn't it? It doesn't matter where customers buy the product they don't want – just give them their money back.

Some people may rip you off unintentionally. Don't think of this as an opportunity to get even with the customer. Think of it as a chance to win a new friend.

For instance, occasionally we had "bad" steaks returned which were bought at a supermarket located right across the street from one of our stores.

We received this note from one of our customers who was angry when he ate a steak which he thought tasted bad:

He said, "I got so mad that I put the steak in a sack and drove over to your store and went to the head clerk at the desk and told him this was the second time this has happened and I'm sick and tired of it."

The angry customer continued, explaining, "Your head clerk said, 'I'm sorry, sir. What would you like, your money back or another steak?' Not only did he give my money back, but he gave me another steak for my trouble." The customer continued, "The next time I get that mad I'm going over to your competition and give them a hard time."

Here was an opportunity for a head clerk to demonstrate a flair for management. He didn't question whether the steak was really bad. Some people will return a perfectly good steak because they didn't happen to like the color or the taste of it, or because they had a fight with their wife. Just accept the return.

The other thing the clerk did not do was question whether the "bad" steak was actually bought from a competitor. So what? The customer thought he had bought the steak at our store and that was good enough for the clerk.

I was proud of this clerk because he put the customer's interest ahead of his desire to "protect" our company from a rip-off artist.

After being treated well, do you think that customer will ever switch?

A meat manager's pride vs. making a customer happy

Your focus should be on doing everything possible to keep your customers happy. If you argue with a customer, you only create ill feelings. But it takes a long time for some employees to realize the wisdom of that approach.

For instance, I discovered that some of our stores' meat market managers had a tough time with our refund policy. Sometimes when a customer brought back a piece of tough meat, managers argued that it was cooked too long or had been left in the car too long before it found its way home.

Whatever the reason, when a complaint presented itself, it was usually more the customer's fault than the meat being defective… according to some of our meat managers.

One day, during a visit to one of our stores, the meat market manager asked me if I could take the time to come into his cutting room. He unwrapped a piece of steak and said, "Look at this steak."

I obeyed. I looked at the steak and said, "It doesn't look that appetizing."

"Do you think I would cut meat like that?"

Knowing he was eventually heading somewhere I played along, saying, "I don't think so."

The meat manager said, "A lady brought that piece of meat back and claimed she bought it here. I gave her the money back. I knew that the woman had bought it from the competition across the street."

I said, "Really? How much refund did you give her?" He said, "$7.56."

I said, "Isn't that great? For the small price of only $7.56, you were able to keep a $5,000 a year customer."

I was being totally serious, but the meat manager didn't appreciate my comment. He thought I was nuts. He was appalled to think that we shouldn't correct the customer.

I explained my thinking to the meat manager. The customer thinks she bought the meat at our store because many customers shop more than one store. We both know she was wrong. But if we argue with the customer, we are basically telling her to leave us and go to a competitor. That doesn't make sense. Why would you send your customers back to your competitor?

This meat manager was not alone in his relationship with customers. I guess what makes great meat managers is pride in their work. But meat managers have to understand that part of their job is making customers want to come back. When they forget that part of their job, they drive me crazy!

One day a woman came into one of our meat markets with a partial ham that she said she claimed had been bought from our store. The woman proceeded to tell our meat manager how much fat was on this ham, saying she wanted her money back.

The market manager said, "Lady, you didn't buy that ham here." Angrily, she said, "I most assuredly did and I want my money back."

"Lady, I will give you your money back. But you didn't buy that ham here."

Luckily for us, the lady gave us a second chance. She wrote a letter to the company describing this event.

We promptly went to the woman's house with a gift certificate as an apology, with the hope that she would forgive us and stay with us as a loyal shopper.

It cost us much more than just giving the woman the refund because we gave her a gift certificate to keep her business.

The meat market manager could have been right about where she purchased the ham. It might not have been purchased in our store. But so what?

Saving money but ruining your business

Let me give you a classic example of how you can ruin your business by being scared of being ripped off. We used to lose an average of two million dollars a year just on bad checks.

One day the controller said, "We need to change our check cashing policy."

"Why?"

"Because we're losing two million a year on bad checks."

"I don't want to lose two million a year. But before you change the policy I want you to add up the number of checks we take in over the next 30 days that are good and the number that are bad and let me see the percentage."

"OK."

It turns out the percentage of checks we took in at our chain that were good was 99.6%. Because our chain's volume was so high, four tenths of a percent made up the two million dollar loss. Should we figure out how to cut the loss down through software and third party solutions? Of course. Should we change our check-cashing policy and make 99.6% of our customers mad? Of course not.

I'm not looking for poor customer service, but . . .

When I tell members of my family I need to return something at a store, they respond with quiet nodding.

Some family members will stare at the ceiling. Others will examine the pattern in the rug. No one volunteers to go along with me to witness the return process, because they know chances are they will see poor customer service.

Here's a typical situation:

I decided to return my Father's Day shirt from my son, which I had only received 24 hours before (it still had the tags on and was wrapped in tissue).

The shirt was a size too large and I just wanted the

same shirt a size smaller. This is what is called an "even exchange."

Sounds easy, doesn't it?

When I reached the shirt counter at the large department store, I stood by the register for at least 15 minutes until someone in sales made eye contact with me.

Then, minutes later, at least two sales people said that the shirt was not "their department" and they could not help me. Finally, someone came along who was in the right department.

I again showed the shirt, the tags and asked for an "even exchange" if they had the same shirt, a size smaller, in stock.

I smiled.

She smiled.

She smiled as she asked me for my driver's license.

I told her the shirt was "for walking and would not be driving."

She was not amused.

I provided the driver's license, all the while thinking that with any luck, we would complete this transaction sometime before the next New Year.

She said, "It's policy."

I tried to hide my amusement, wondering what moron wrote this into a policy manual.

The sales clerk tried to make conversation as she completed the transaction.

She was not kidding when she said, "You are very lucky that this shirt is still on sale. Otherwise, you would have to pay the difference between the sale price and the retail price."

That was in the manual, too.

Was this transaction listed in the manual under the heading of "How not to develop a loyal relationship with the customer" or "How can I not help you?"

The lesson here is that an organization can have a policy manual with policies listed. However, the first rule in the manual should be: If any policy in this manual conflicts with your common sense, trust your common sense!

The sales clerk is in the driver's seat when it comes to relationship building and bonding with the customer. She can very easily turn a customer off, or, with a better attitude, create a loyal customer for life.

Treating all customers equally

Just as annoying as employees who don't use common sense are employees who display an attitude to customers they deem "inferior."

I always impressed upon our employees that it was important to treat every customer, including food stamp customers, alike.

People who shop using food stamps are still customers and deserve as much respect as any other customers who choose us for their shopping.

One of our employees who saw a customer driving an upscale car "had" to tell other employees, and other customers, that the same customer had just used food stamps to pay for her purchase.

This is outrageous behavior.

We never know the circumstances of our shoppers; the woman could have just lost her job, or she could be a single mother who needs help... who knows?

Is her story any of our business or is it our business to share that woman's business with others?

No. It is gossip.

Chances are that when we gossip about the customers, our behavior matches our attitude. We are not treating these customers with the dignity they deserve.

If these customers don't get dignity from us when shopping with food stamps, they won't take their non-food stamp business to us when and if their circumstances change.

I only want people working in my organization who give the benefit of the doubt to everyone who walks through our doors. All our customers should be treated like honored guests.

CHAPTER

3

How to Stop the Switchers

Here is my belief. All your customers, even your satisfied customers, are candidates for switching.

Your competitors are waiting with open arms to welcome your customers. They are enticing your customers with sales, with new products and even with special incentives for switching. You won't keep all your customers, no matter what you do. Customers like to keep their options open.

I know I do.

I admit it. Even though I try to be a loyal customer, I will switch loyalties if I receive exceptional service.

From 1982 to 1990, I was on an airplane almost daily. In those days, I mostly flew United or Continental Airlines, because their routes matched my travel schedule. Because of the airlines' frequent flyer programs I was able to earn bonus miles that could be traded for free trips or upgrades to first class.

The additional room in first class provided a better, quieter work atmosphere where I could spread papers around and catch up on reading.

Continental and United had reeled me in with their loyalty programs, and despite all my trips, I had not used another airline service for more than eight years.

One day I planned a trip to Dallas, Texas with a return flight to Denver that same evening. The only way

I could manage to stay within my travel plans was to leave Denver at 6:00 a.m. on American Airlines. I was a bit upset not to be taking Continental or United, but I had no choice.

On the morning of my trip, I arrived at the ticket counter early. Just as I was planning to check in, I asked the young representative behind the counter if the airline offered a "miles club."

"Yes, we do, and would you want to enroll this morning?"

I told her I would and asked her if her program was like that of United's, in which, after accumulating 10,000 miles, the traveler could upgrade to first class for only $20 or like Continental's, which allowed for a FREE upgrade to first class after one accumulated a certain number of miles.

The travel agent politely asked, "Do you want to upgrade this morning?"

"Yes, but sadly, I do not have any accumulated mileage."

She did not refer to a book of policies. Nor did she reach out to a higher-level decision maker. She simply said, "That's okay. You are a first time traveler. I'll upgrade you for $20."

I pulled out a $20 bill before she changed her mind or the airlines changed shifts.

She rapidly completed the paperwork. As I was leaving the ticket counter, I complimented her on her kind offer. She called me back to the counter.

She said, "Just a minute, please. I noticed that you are scheduled to return this afternoon on Continental Airlines."

Now, I was sure we were both remembering what I told her earlier, that Continental had already upgraded me to first class FREE. I told her that was the plan.

She said, "We have a plane that leaves one hour later than you are now scheduled to leave… and, if you agree to wait for our flight, I will upgrade you free."

I was entranced. I love it when customer service goes beyond the expected to benefit the customer. I booked the return flight on American.

I left the counter reveling in good customer service feelings. Only later did I realize what I had done. I was already booked on first class and now I had to wait an extra hour than originally planned because of what the representative was able to do for me! Waiting the extra hour for this was not my best choice since I already was on first class, but I did it because I had received such terrific customer service.

The service on the flights was great both ways. Two weeks later, when I booked a flight to Chicago, can you guess which airline I called?

American Airlines, of course.

Two weeks after that I had to go to Cincinnati. Guess how I went? American Airlines.

Now, here is the point – neither Continental Airlines or United Airlines did anything wrong. But they did not do enough to keep me from switching!

To this day, I am not sure that American Airlines' service was any better than the others were, but I perceived it to be, due to the work of the nice ticket representative.

How the casino industry works to prevent switching

The casino industry does a far better job than most industries in realizing the propensity of customers to switch and doing something about it.

Casinos do have frequent player programs that reward their customers in a similar way that airlines reward frequent flyers. Play the slots for a couple of hours and you may earn a meal. Play the slots for two days and your room might be comped. Play five dollars a pull and you will be treated like a high roller.

Yet the casinos realize their competitors offer the same advantages. To keep their customers loyal, the casinos work extra hard. They may have a slots tournament with free admission for their top players. They may have world class entertainment with free front row seats for the top players. Birthday gifts are common. The more you play, the more attention you receive.

And the more the casinos treat their top customers like royalty, the less likely they will have mass defections.

Despite what you do, there's no stopping some people from switching from you to a competitor. You can't stop all the switching, so don't worry about some defections. And there's another factor at work which should make you breathe a little easier. Most customers aren't looking to switch. If you keep your customers happy, if your products are good, if your service is outstanding and if your policies make sense, most customers will stay with you.

A crisis on Thanksgiving morning

Sometimes you have to go far beyond merely refunding a small amount of money or giving a gift certificate to keep customers from switching. And when you do so, you can create a whole family of tremendously appreciative and loyal customers.

Some years ago, a customer from one of our stores had purchased a turkey and all the necessary side dishes to feed a family of fourteen for Thanksgiving.

When she started to cook the turkey on Thanksgiving morning, it was sour. At that time, our store and all the supermarkets in the area were closed on Thanksgiving.

There was no place our customer could buy another turkey and start dinner over. The family of fourteen was soon to arrive with hearty appetites.

This was a crisis.

Despite the time crunch that would have halted a lesser person in her tracks, this woman was resourceful. She called Ray Rose, who was the president of the company at the time. Ray's actions made a tremendous impression on me and my colleagues, and we still tell this story all the time.

Ray always listed his telephone number in the phone book. He picked up the ringing phone, thinking it was another relative calling to wish his family a happy holiday, when his mood was interrupted by her screeching voice.

She was madder than you know what.

The woman regained her composure and proceeded to tell Ray that she was expecting fourteen guests for turkey dinner and had no turkey. She was offering to hold him personally responsible because "your store's turkey was sour."

Of course it was possible that the woman had left the turkey out too long and that's why it had turned sour. It was also possible she hadn't even bought the turkey at our store. But it certainly wasn't the time to interrogate an obviously irate customer.

Ray apologized – and told her she should take the fourteen people out to dinner at any restaurant she chose and send him the bill.

The total bill was $375 including the tip. I'm sure our accountants and a lot of our associates thought he was crazy.

But can you guess how many people our customer told this story to?

$375 is cheap advertising! Keeping a family happy on Thanksgiving is priceless.

Unique solutions to problems

Sometimes an employee's creativity can solve a problem that doesn't have a solution in the policy manual.

Our stores sold numerous general merchandise items over the years but had not sold appliances in over five years.

One day a woman brought back a clock radio that she claimed she had purchased from us two years ago and now, two years later, she wanted her money back.

The manager said, "Really? How much did you pay for it?"

She said, "$29."

The manager returned the money to the woman, put the radio on the shelf and sold it for $32.

This is not rocket science.

Just do it and keep those customers coming back for more.

When trust is as important as price

Building customer loyalty can discourage switching. It can even discourage people from thinking about switching.

I found that some loyal customers would not even go to a competitor's grand opening, when the initial sales offers are tremendous bargains. They didn't want to go anywhere where the "shopping feel" was not right.

A discount warehouse store opened right next door to one of our stores. It had much lower labor rates than we did and, as a result, the store offered lower prices.

In fact, any of our customers could walk across our parking lot to the other store's parking lot – the competition was that close. When compared to our prices, item by item, the other store was 10% less.

Yet even though our weekly volume dipped when the low price competitor located in our neighborhood, we still managed to do a lot of business.

Customers chose us because of all that we offered to make the shopping experience better for the shopper. We had a no-questions-asked refund policy, we encouraged special orders, we had free cookies for kids, more variety in products and employees who went out of their way to help customers. Price is important, but it is not the only reason customers shop with you.

Some stores are lured into the price game of "How low can you go?" If the lowest price was always the reason for a customer's shopping decision, the low price leader would have all the business.

They don't, and that's because for many customers comfort, reliability and trust are as important to them as price.

Looking for customer service problems

Whenever anyone talks about a poor customer experience, I become very interested.

My wife and I were having lunch at a little café near one of our stores when I overheard a man in the next booth relay a "bad shopping experience" story to the person with whom he was lunching. The listening audience widened as it now included the waiter who was serving the man, along with others who also overheard the story just by being near the booth and eavesdropping on them. Bad stories can stop traffic.

Fortunately, the bad shopping experience as told by the customer in the nearby booth did not happen at one of our stores. It happened at the store of the competition located just across the street.

As I acknowledged this man's story of woe and indignation, I removed a coupon from a book we had put together to apologize for bad service at our store. I introduced myself and told the man I hoped his day would be better and as an apology for the poor service he received, gave him a coupon redeemable at our store.

The man was caught by surprise but said that this was

one "apology for bad service" that would not be forgotten.

Did this won-over customer walk right out and go to our store to shop? That I don't know. But, I do know this – that in his mind, he will connect good customer service to our organization.

This was not an unusual situation. It seems that every day I hear multiple tales of poor customer service. Partially, this is because people know of my passion for customer service and love to tell me their tales of woe. But it is also because there are so many people who are subjected to poor customer service they have to tell someone.

People also seek me out to tell me when they perceive they have received good service.

A store manager recently told me her family had a problem with their snow blower because it was leaking gas. She related to me how she called the supplier and the supplier told her how they were short-handed, but for her to go ahead and call someone to fix it and to send the bill him.

She thought that was great service. I said "You don't suppose the supplier should have called someone for you?" She stopped for a second and then said, "You're right. I still don't realize when service isn't what it ought to be."

Why You Should Solicit Customer Complaints

I love customer complaints!

You should, too. To see why, just consider the alternatives when one of your customers is unhappy with your business:

• She can tell her friends and neighbors as well as random people she meets on the street how awful your business is;

• She can be so upset she stops shopping with you and never comes back; or

• She can complain and let you try to make things right.

Of the three alternatives the customer has, only the third gives you an opportunity to make her happy. In some cases, you can turn a complaint upside down and create a very loyal customer.

One day I was sitting in my office and my phone rang. Just as soon as I answered the phone, a customer started yelling at me.

He was upset over an incident that happened in one of our stores. The man was yelling so loudly that I held the phone receiver five inches from my ear to avoid permanent hearing loss.

I listened.

He continued to yell.

When he wore down a bit and paused to catch his breath, I took advantage of the opportunity to get a word into the conversation.

I said, "Mr. Parks, I'm surprised you're not madder."

Dead silence.

I said, "I have to apologize. We obviously have done a poor job of training."

He said, "Oh no, it's not your fault," in a quiet voice.

He was on my side now. I said, "Yes, that employee thinks what he did was right and that is really our fault. Give me your address - we'll take care of this right away."

Within the hour, a manager arrived at his house with a gift certificate, an apology and a business card.

The important thing to understand is I did not even know if what Mr. Parks said was true. I didn't even investigate his complaint right away.

Mr. Parks obviously was so upset that he had to call the president of the company. My job was to make him happy. There would be time down the road to talk to people about what had upset Mr. Parks and to make any necessary changes in our policies and procedures.

The first thing that had to be done was to make Mr. Parks happy.

I have always told our people that the best way to handle an irate customer or any irate person is to do the following: When people are mad, and I mean <u>really</u> mad … the first thing you do is AGREE with them. It drives them nuts! By agreeing with them, you will often immediately calm them down and together you can work out any problems.

To fix a complaint, you don't have to wait until a

customer actually calls you or shows up at your door. If you find out about a problem, you can be proactive.

A few years ago, I gave a presentation about customer service to our accounting department.

After the meeting, an employee told me that her neighbor had quit shopping with us because she tried to cash a check and we "gave her a bad time" when we refused to cash her check.

Her neighbor had never been back to our store. That night I had the store manager show up at the neighbor's house with an apology, a gift certificate and a request that the woman give us another chance.

She was surprised by our effort to correct our behavior and said she would try us again.

The next day, the young woman from the accounting department came into my office to tell me that she could not believe what we did. Her neighbor had come over to her house after the manager had been there just to let her know how surprised she was and to relay the story.

The point here is that even our own employee did not know how serious we were about improving our customer service. Once employees see that owners and managers care deeply about each customer, they are quick to follow the lead.

The benefit of customer comment cards

One way to institutionalize response to customer complaints is to institute a customer comment system. Many companies have them, but I think ours is unique.

At each of our stores, we featured a convenient holder at checkout stands, filled with customer comment cards. We had a captive audience at the checkout areas, especially at peak busy times. Not only were the cards available but they were stamped prepaid and the return address was to the president – me.

The comment cards were easy to fill out, but we wanted the customers to tell us exactly why they were pleased or upset with us so we had lines for comments rather than check-off boxes. I felt that rating stores by good, bad, great, excellent, poor or another choice in between would not really describe the customer's experience. Ratings of good, bad, great, excellent or poor will never tell a manager exactly how to improve on weaknesses and expand on strengths. These answers are not specific enough.

I believe that a customer would prefer to write out her comments as opposed to checking off boxes.

Customers would write compliments on these cards as well as complaints. Our system was such that EVERY card, regardless if it was a compliment or complaint, earned a phone call from one of the management teams within the store.

In some companies, the personnel or public relations departments are responsible for sorting and acknowledging complaints or compliments. With that kind of system, it takes a while for comments of any kind to filter through. And, when the comments are finally reported to top management, they are so diluted that it is difficult to take any action.

In that type of system, the customer may receive a response but it is usually in the form of a cold letter that is not personally signed. These form letters rarely respond to the specific comment but instead promote store policies.

Think about it.

Your customer never shops your store via the personnel or public relations department. It does not make sense that a response to a customer comment should come from a department that has little front line contact and no power to resolve complaints in a rapid manner. By the time the customer receives a form letter, the complaint is forgotten and the customer has moved on – probably to shop your competition.

Timing is everything.

When managers handle complaints on a personal and direct level, there is a chance to change anger and frustration to loyalty. If we received a complaint that demonstrated that the customer was very upset, then the managers would just show up at the customer's residence with an apology cake, a certificate, and information on what we would do to correct the problem.

The formerly irate customer could see that people in the store really cared about her.

We generally received around 1,500 to 2,000 comment cards per week that we would forward back to the original stores for processing.

The manager of each location would fill out a form describing how the situation was resolved.

The comment cards and the written response were forwarded to the district manager, who would read the store manager's response to be sure that the issue was handled properly.

The cards would come into the office and every day my secretary would randomly place at least twenty cards on my desk for reading and evaluating, give twenty cards to the executive vice president and another twenty to the vice president of marketing.

Think about it – sixty cards a day, over three hundred cards a week were read by the top three managers in the organization. When a card was not handled in a way that we thought was right, it went back to the store so that the manager could correct any problem and learn how to handle a similar situation should it arise again.

I cannot tell you how valuable that activity was for our organization and for our employees in confidence building.

I couldn't possibly read all of the comment cards, but our managers always routed the cards to me that started with, "Dear Don, you probably won't read this, but I'm writing anyway."

You can't believe the customer's response to a personal call from the president, especially when there were no expectations of getting that high up the ladder.

In addition, we coded the cards by positive or negative comments and by the department identified in the cards. In this way, we were able to monitor how many complaints or compliments we received on a department for each store.

For example, after one thirteen-week period, we received four complaints on the deli department in store #8. That number of complaints is always a reason for concern. Our procedure was to have the district manager review the cards with the department. Then, the department would institute a set of procedures to cut down the number of complaints in the future.

Another benefit of using comment cards is the opportunity for creating future sales. Our store managers had "carte blanche" when taking care of the customer. When these managers talked with customers on the phone, the personalized contact gave our managers a chance to ask customers about our strengths and weaknesses so that we could improve what we needed to make better and maintain what customers liked.

We would ask customers what they would like to see us add in the way of products and services as well as services or products we should omit.

Our marketing strategy was to provide customers more of what they wanted and less of what they didn't.

During one time period we recorded having received 48% positive cards and 52% negative cards. In a few years, we were able to reverse those numbers and the balance changed to 48% negative and 52% positive.

My staff used to ask me, "What do you want – 100% positive comments?"

"Yes," I said. "You want to know why? Because if we don't set the bar at 100%, we'll never get much better than we are now. For example, if you flew on an airline that had 1% of its flights crash, would you continue to fly? What is the accepted rate of newborns dropped in a nursery at a hospital? We can't afford to settle for having one newborn baby dropped. That's the approach I want our employees to take for customer service in our stores."

Some companies try everything to monitor the customer service provided by employees. Some use "mystery shoppers," who are pretend shoppers who are actually monitoring employee behavior, to give reports on employee service to management.

I think companies that use mystery shoppers are making a big mistake. It's like you are spying on your employees. How do you think employees feel when they find you have sent in a mystery shopper? They feel like you don't trust them.

And why do we send the mystery shoppers only to evaluate the behavior of front-line employees? Why not send the mystery shopper to check up on the employees in the personnel department or public relations department – the people who dreamed up this idea?

Why not send a mystery shopper to check on the vice-president of operations, or better yet the president and have the mystery shopper send the report to the board of directors noting his or her activities?

We don't do it because it would be embarrassing. But management doesn't care as much about embarrassing front-line employees. If you really want a team, then everyone should work together.

A system such as customer comment cards gives honest feedback from real customers. A mystery shopper is just someone who is paid to find mistakes. Funny, isn't it – companies pay mystery shoppers with no affiliation to the company and read their report like it's "gospel," but won't spend time reading their own customers' comment cards, which are real feedback.

Postpone investigations

Handling complaints first and then doing investigations later removes a lot of headaches from the system.

I remember an incident at checkout which made it clear why we don't question customers' complaints, especially in front of other customers. I happened to be in the store that day and observed the customer service desk.

The checkout line at customer service was long that day, consisting of seven or eight customers holding bags of items they wanted to return.

At the front of the line was a man holding a chicken wrapped in plastic. He was holding this chicken at arms' length. The man unwrapped the chicken and handed it to the assistant manager.

With outstretched arms, the customer said, "Here. This is your chicken."

The assistant manager wore a furrowed brow and was trying to display empathy. She was tuned in, giving the impression that she was listening using body language that was supposed to lend a air of confidence to the customer.

She wore the "you can trust me because I am wearing the badge of an assistant manager" look.

The man produced a receipt for the cooked chicken, which was now starting to smell. The man explained how he had tried to serve the chicken for dinner when it fell apart to the touch.

The meat fell off the bones and the bones fell away from the midsection of the chicken. The chicken skin did not fare better as it seemed to disintegrate. The man had decided to return the chicken to the store.

Here is where my story becomes fun.

The assistant manager, who took her job to heart (it would have been better if she took her job to her head), said, "Well, it doesn't look that bad to me."

She smelled the chicken in areas that hinted at something beyond casual friendship.

She took the chicken and showed it to each person down the line saying, "Here, you smell it. It doesn't seem that bad, does it?"

The waiting customers were a cooperative lot. They kindly took their turns at smelling this chicken that now looked like a pile of chicken mush from all the handling. Each person in the line took a turn sniffing and commenting – shaking heads and shrugging shoulders. My physician doesn't give me such a complete examination when I go in for my annual physical. I was about to give this manager a lesson in customer service when I spotted her supervisor heading our way with plans to correct the situation.

The supervisor said, "Just give this man his money back and offer him another chicken."

The supervisor was fortunate.

He could lend his opinion and supervise without having to smell the chicken.

The customer was happy to have his money back and to be able to leave the chicken behind. He opted not to try his luck with another chicken.

Having all our customers (who were already waiting to return merchandise) touch and smell a marginal chicken is not a recipe for customer service success.

Communicating with customers

I am excited whenever I see an example of a marketing strategy that can reduce the number of customers with unsatisfied complaints.

In Boston, one restaurant requests that their staff hand write notes to customers who have dined with them, thanking them for their business and expressing the hope that the dining experience was good. The restaurant also gives a phone number for customers who have any questions or complaints.

Now, this marketing strategy is not used as a means of torturing the staff into developing their note-writing skills. It is a great example of how to institute a personalized quality control system.

This is a true grass-roots customer service program. The notes demonstrate personal attention. The restaurant hopes that this quality of personal attention will help them stand apart from all their competitors that do not pay extra attention to customers frequenting their restaurants.

Personal attention goes a long way, especially when the standard is no appreciation.

When the steak is tough, the stakes are high

I'm always on the lookout for examples of good – and bad – customer service.

My wife and I attended a service club dinner and prepared to sit through a long night of awards and "thank you so much" speeches. We were at a table set for ten.

Following the introductions of all those at the table, we proceeded to share with one another what we do in the business sector when we are not helping non-profit groups.

The meal consisted of steak, vegetables and mashed potatoes. The woman just to my right began to cut into her steak. She moved the dinner knife from one position to another on the steak, trying to get a grip on the meat with her fork so that she could make the initial clean cut with the dinner knife.

The woman spoke to me, saying, "I can't cut my steak."

Everyone offered her a piece of steak, including me. She declined, telling us that she needed to cut her own steak. The man next to me, who was interested in what was happening, commented that his steak was also very tough.

When a server came to our table to ask if everything was okay, the woman informed her of her dilemma – which was that the steak could not be cut.

The server thought for a moment, eyes rolling upward for that answer that would fix everything, paused, smiled and then answered, "Perhaps you need a sharper knife."

My wife nudged me with the special signal between husbands and wives that means "listen but resist turning this into instruction on customer service."

I watched the woman to my right as her facial expression turned to shock. Steam started to leak from her ears and she finally spoke to the server. "Why would I need a different knife than these other people who are eating the same thing? The man over there (she pointed to the man just to my left) has the same problem – overdone steak.

"Why don't you take this meat back and make shoes out of it? Just get me a piece of steak I can cut. You need not bring me a saw for my meat."

The server said, "Well, if we don't go the sharper knife route, chef will have to cook a new steak and that will take at least 15 to 20 minutes. You'll be eating your meat when everyone else is on dessert."

She chose the steak and said she "would wait until midnight, if it took that long" because she was sure the speeches would take that long.

The server shrugged.

The man to my left with the overdone steak was quiet through all this. He let the woman to my right do the talking for the both of them. She was the louder of the two, voicing her complaints, punctuated with hand gestures.

There is an interesting point here. The server paid more attention to the louder of the two complainers. However, the quieter of the two, the man to my left, had just been elected as chairperson for the next year's meeting of that organization. He would be in charge of choosing the hotel for next year's event as well as the menu for the same. She should have paid attention to both people and given them a little customer service. Because of the server's poor service and poor judgment, there was very little chance that next year's meeting would take place at the same hotel.

I'm sure most people, if they think about it a little, realize they've been subjected to many bad cases of customer service. I'm sure most people can think of a story or two where a business didn't take care of them properly.

You can't control poor customer service at other businesses, but you can try to stem it at your own.

Part II
Employees

CHAPTER

5

Employees as Super Heroes

Meet my employees: the new Justice League of America!

You might remember the old Justice League of America. It consisted of Superman and all of his pals – Batman, Flash, Green Lantern and Wonder Woman. These Super Heroes would band together to fight evil and help people throughout the world.

We wanted to encourage our own Super Heroes to help people throughout our stores. In our organization we called these employees "Quiet Heroes" because they gave great service without a lot of fanfare. To do so, we offered programs to reward employees for providing good customer service.

When we received a letter or comment complimenting one of our employees, we saved it. At the end of the year, employees and managers voted on the top five stories and selected the best. We awarded one hundred shares of our stock to the employee who won. More important than the prizes was the recognition these employees received. Our emphasis on finding Quiet Heroes let all our employees know we encouraged and rewarded great customer service.

The first employee who won a Quiet Hero award was a floral department manager at one of our supermarkets.

I found out about this employee when I received a letter from an attorney. If you're like me, you get a little nervous when you see a letter from a law firm. I relaxed a little when I started reading.

The attorney's letter explained that his sixteen-year-old daughter was recently invited to her very first dance. The Friday night before the dance, the attorney's daughter's date called to cancel. His daughter was devastated.

The attorney and his wife were upset because their daughter was hurt. This was their little girl's first big date and now it was cancelled.

The attorney continued, "I got up the next morning and told my wife I'm going over and get our daughter a nice gift from your store's floral department."

"I went in and met your floral department manager, Nancy, and I told her my story. I had never met her before. Nancy could not believe what had happened to my daughter. She showed more empathy than you can imagine. She told me to come back in two hours and promised she would have something nice.

"I came back in two hours later and paid for the arrangement. When I got home, my phone rang. It was Nancy. She told me that a courtesy clerk who worked at the store also went to my daughter's high school. She added that he agreed to take my daughter to the dance. Not only did she arrange for the date but she also took up a collection from the other employees to pay for my daughter's corsage and the dinner for the couple.

"By the way – the couple is still dating."

Nancy did not ask a supervisor, did not ask the manager, she just helped the customer on her own.

When you create a climate for employees to feel safe to take action and they know they will not get in trouble if their intentions are to take care of the customer, they will transform themselves into Quiet Heroes.

The reasons behind the policy

You know you have a Quiet Hero when an employee understands the reasons behind company policy. This type of employee can rise above a strict interpretation of the rules because they understand the spirit of the policy.

It's been our company policy for years to give a free cookie to little kids.

Some supermarkets have a cookie club where a card must be presented in order to obtain a cookie.

I don't like that idea because when a child shows up at the cookie counter, I don't want the employees to say, "Sorry. No card. No cookie."

Our company's program was to give children a cookie when they asked for one.

One night, one of our produce warehouse forklift operators was standing behind a dad and his two little girls at the bakery counter. The girls' faces pressed against the glass as they selected their favorite cookie.

It was late, near dinnertime and the family was tired after a long day. The cookie counter was the last stop before check out.

One little girl pointed to a cookie while telling the clerk, "I want that one." The clerk insisted, "That's not the free one. The free one is in the other case, over there."

The children did not want the free cookie that was offered. Suddenly, a deep voice from behind the dad, the forklift operator, interrupted the exchange by saying, "Give the girls the cookies they want. I'll pay for them."

The dad told the forklift operator that he should not do that. The forklift operator responded with, "Sir, I'm an employee of this company and our policy is to give children the cookies they want."

The forklift operator paid for the cookies.

Now, I don't blame the bakery clerk. She was doing what she had been told to do. In her training class, she learned the location of the FREE cookies. No one ever said what should happen if a child wanted a different cookie. But the forklift operator was a Quiet Hero. He understood the reason for the cookie policy: to make little kids and their parents happy. This was the kind of employee attitude we tried to encourage.

A whole store understands good customer service

Good customer service can be catching. If one employee in a store shows outstanding customer service and is rewarded or commended for her efforts, her colleagues start to pitch in to show that they also know how to take care of customers.

I recall receiving a letter from a customer who was truly overwhelmed at the honest and sincere attention he had received at one of our stores. This customer said that, on more than one occasion, this store had given exceptional customer service beyond the call of duty.

He wrote, "Last night at 10:00 p.m. this store demonstrated exceptional service once again. My daughter has been ill and couldn't take Tylenol orally to reduce her rising fever, so the doctor recommended suppositories. When there were none available at this store, the staff jumped to my assistance. One employee ran across the street to the competition to see if they had any. They told me, 'If they don't have it, we will try other stores until we find it.'"

The customer continued, "... During one store visit, I was buying rock salt and I needed one more bag. The store manager had one of the clerks run across the street to Safeway to buy it for me.

"During another store visit, a moving shopping cart hit my wife's car. When I told the store manager about the accident, he said, 'No problem, please have the damage estimated and we'll have it repaired.'

"Another time, when I was in the store's check out line, a soda can exploded. The can exploded when the clerk was checking out the groceries. As the can hit the side of my cart, it sprayed sugary soda all over me. The manager, seeing this, apologized and gave me a $50 certificate for food.

"Your pharmacist, Sandy, was delivering a prescription to our home when a little girl who was playing with our daughter ran into a wall, cutting her head open. Sandy quickly assisted and helped stop the bleeding until we could get additional emergency care.

"I could go on and on. The people at this store have completely won my trust, my business, my loyalty and my appreciation as people who care about their business and the customer.

"The stories are like a Norman Rockwell *Saturday Evening Post* painting of Americana in days gone by; days that we wish were still here. Well, that feeling is captured at this store and by your people. Good attitude abounds in this store. It is something that's missed so much in today's busy world."

When you receive a letter like that, you know that your company is doing something right.

I read these letters and told other employees about these Quiet Heroes in staff meetings. I wanted our employees to know it is okay to use their imagination in solving customer problems. The best employees, the Quiet Heroes, go beyond what they are required to do to help out customers who are in need.

Understanding a customer's special needs

Here is another letter I received that illustrates unusual employee performance.

"I am writing to tell you of an employee who deserves your highest commendation, based on a rather extraordinary experience I had Sunday, August 25th.

"Your employee's name is Tom, and he is a head clerk at one of your stores. It will take some explaining to help you understand how far above and beyond the call of duty Tom went for me.

"On Sunday, I planned my activities very carefully as I was scheduled to have surgery four days later and was short on energy and time to get things done prior to surgery.

"One of my tasks was to take care of buying a birthday present for my son, who lives in Los Angeles. Getting the gift ready to ship the next day put some pressure on me, in light of my surgery and limited time schedule. The other task was to get plenty of groceries to take us though the week and past my surgery date.

"My plan was to go to the leather goods store for the birthday gift and then to your store for groceries.

"I bought the birthday gift, which consisted of a silver buckle set, a leather belt, and two western shirts – each costing normally $45. However, the shirts were on sale that day for only $20 each. I put the package in the trunk of my Cadillac and then went to your store for my groceries. I checked out my groceries, had them sacked in plastic and loaded them into my trunk.

"When I got home and unloaded the groceries, I discovered that the strong bleach product, Tilex, must have had a loose lid. The plastic bag it was in (along with some rice) was swimming in bleach and the bottle was now empty. The sack had leaked on the clothing I was wearing, soaked my car trunk, and gone through part of the western store sack, ruining the two shirts, which were part of my son's birthday gift.

"Of the groceries, only the box of rice was ruined. I called the store and talked with Tom, the head clerk. I knew that you would replace the grocery products. Tom assured me of that. I even figured you would pay me for the loss of the shirts. Tom assured me of that too.

"However, your store's Tom did more than that.
"HE HEARD ME.

"He heard me when I said that I didn't want to recover damages I didn't deserve, but that these were unusual circumstances for me; four days before surgery, with no more time to shop for my son's birthday gift. Could I even find high quality shirts at the same sale prices again? It all seemed hopeless.

"Tom came to my house not once, but twice that evening. He picked up the ruined shirts, the clothing I had been wearing, and the receipt from the western store, which showed both the original price and the sale price of the shirts. He came back with the replacements for the grocery products, cash to compensate me for the original price of the shirts, and an offer to send my birthday present to my son via UPS, at no charge to me.

"As a professional person myself, I would say that your Tom has a great future with you. In addition, if we can clone him, I have a few clients who will take a dozen or so.

"Thank you for creating the kind of environment that makes Tom take the kind of initiative he did on behalf of a customer. It certainly has renewed my faith in the phrase 'Customer Service.'"

All employees are able to deliver outstanding service

Common sense is not restricted to any one group of people. A cashier can often exhibit better people skills than the owner of a company. I've found that some clerks and assistant managers are far better able to handle a problem than their superiors. Consider this letter I received from a customer:

"On Friday, I had a dinner party at my house for some friends and business clients. I stopped by your store around 5:30 pm that evening to pick up some items that I needed for the dinner party. When I went to the produce department for the produce I needed, I discovered that the store was completely out of green onions.

"I asked a clerk in that department if there were any

green onions available and he stated they were out and returned to his duties. I then approached the manager's station and asked why they were out of green onions and was told that 'people were buying green onions like crazy and he just didn't know why.'

"After checking out, I again stopped by the manager's station and told the assistant manager that the answer I had received from him was the most stupid answer I had ever heard. He stated that he would call another store to see if they had any green onions, but I told him that wouldn't help me because I needed them now. I then left the store thinking how I had been inconvenienced again because the store had run out of an item I needed.

"At 6:30 pm that evening I was surprised to find your assistant manager at my home. He was delivering four packages of green onions and not only did he apologize for what had happened, but also resold me on that store. He informed me that this particular incident was not indicative of the store and that the people employed there were really interested in taking care of their customers."

Another letter written to our president some years ago is another example of what it means to give superior service, not average service.

It reads: "In this day and age it is a rare occasion for someone to go out of their way to make another's life a little more enjoyable. Your company should be proud of the fact they do employ such a person.

"August 5th was my mother's 80th birthday and I had invited 20 relatives over for a party to help her celebrate the occasion. I had ordered a birthday cake two weeks in advance in person at your store. Never doubting that the cake would be there the day of the party, I went in to pick it up – but no cake. No invoice could be found to prove that I had even ordered it. I did have a copy at home but not with me. The bakery girl made a quick phone call to the central bakery and then said, sorry, no cake order had been received. I wanted to cry right there. My mother is in a nursing home and we were on our way to pick her up for her party and we had no cake to give her.

"The bakery girl gave me a ready-made cake with a sugar "Happy Birthday" on it and ugly mixed up flowers and said that's all she could do.

"When I got home, I phoned another one of your stores to see if they had received my cake by mistake. No cake there either, but the lady said she would try to do something for me. Very shortly, I received a call from your bakery supervisor. I told her my story and she promised me that before my party a cake would be decorated and delivered to my house.

"Within 1-1/2 hours my cake was delivered to the door, exactly as I had ordered it.

"I can't imagine going through with that party (maybe my mother's last) without a special cake for her.

"I thoroughly support your slogan 'Our People Make the Difference,' and I find it very refreshing to know there are still people who think a simple birthday cake is important enough to someone to take the time to see that I had one."

All these incidents are not earth-shattering. People give ordinary birthday cakes all the time, kids break dates, grocery items often leak in a trunk. But the people who experience these events are very affected by these seemingly trivial occurrences. When an employee has the empathy and sense to help a person who suffers through these annoyances, that employee is not only helping the customer, he is providing a great example to his fellow employees.

These incidents of helping individual customers do make an impact. But we decided to see if we could also make a difference in the larger community.

Making an impact in the community

When I was first named president of my organization, I felt pride in the reputation that our company had earned within the communities we served. I felt that our service, collectively, was unequaled by any other business. But it didn't seem like enough.

I thought we could work harder to do better.

I wanted to create a "family of workers." This sense of a "family away from home" would give our employees a safe, enjoyable place to work, where they felt that management cared about employees as much as the "bottom line."

Still searching for a project worthy of conveying this theme, I challenged those around me. That challenge was met by one of our employees who designed a special project called H.O.P.E.

H.O.P.E. stands for "Helping Other People Emerge."

It was a company-wide volunteer community project initiated by us and our family of employees. This umbrella program focused on two types of needs.

The first, Emergency Need, addressed the need of providing support to shelters, food banks, and emergency aid centers within the communities we served.

The second focus, Educational Need, was the establishment of community-wide educational partnerships and scholarships.

Emergency Needs: Within the area of Emergency Needs, we identified specific agencies and shelters that coincided with the geographical area of the employees' workplace. The workplace then adopted and supported these agencies with volunteer employees. Our task was to find ways to enhance customer awareness of the emergency need resources available within their community as well as the need for food, clothing, financial support and volunteers.

Educational Needs: The issues of literacy and school drop out rates were concerns of our educational institutions, the business sector, parents and community members. Our organizations' H.O.P.E. for education was designed to establish mentorship relations, education partnerships and goal achievement for our young people. Within these education partnerships was the opportunity for company volunteers to truly impact and enhance the educational process of children, while having a rewarding and meaningful experience.

These activities began a scheduled "Year of H.O.P.E.," presented by our organization and its employees. Every store and support facility had a H.O.P.E. Committee and each adopted their own project, without management interference.

Over time, the employees were supporting sixty-five to seventy needy organizations – all as community volunteers. A group of employees from one of our stores demonstrated an example of program success. This group organized volunteers who spent a weekend planting flowers and cleaning up the grounds on a home for abused children. In addition, staff planned a barbecue for the children and the faculty.

Another example of this community outreach was demonstrated when one of our store's volunteers from the meat processing plant and Teamsters from our distribution center painted and fixed up homes for the elderly in a low-income neighborhood.

A group of our Teamsters organized another project. They painted a home for single moms that was managed by a rescue mission. They also put in a sprinkler system and fencing for this home.

People want to help others.

They just need to know what to do and need to hold the belief that the work is better when completed as a team. Our employees collaborated with one another. People in our communities benefited, including our employees, whose pride at work escalated as a direct result of this program.

A hungry family

The following story is important to me. It shows what employees will do and how far they will go when they are empowered to take care of customers without fear of consequences if they make a mistake.

The city was Denver.

The year was 1994.

The month was January.

The temperature was 17 below zero.

When it gets that cold in Denver, the shelters fill up and the homeless have nowhere to go. One such homeless woman, with her three children ages nine, eleven and twelve drove all the way to Denver from Los Angeles with the hope of finding a place to live and a new job.

This young mother had been working for a 7-11 store in the Los Angeles area. After she and her three children had settled in Denver, her husband would join them.

However, when the woman arrived in Denver, she was out of money, the shelters were full and she and her children had absolutely nowhere to go. This family was simply out of luck.

Not only was the family out of luck but they were hungry. So, the woman sent her oldest two boys into our downtown store to steal food because they had run out of options.

The boys were caught stealing.

Our security department, along with the assistant manager took the two shaking-in-their-boots boys upstairs to interview them. The boys were crying uncontrollably, barely able to speak. The assistant manager asked the boys about their parents. The boys finally told the staff that their mother was in the car outside the store waiting for them to return.

The assistant manager went outside, located the mother and noticed that she had a third son – a nine-year-old who was clutching onto his mother's sleeve.

The assistant manager asked the mother to join them upstairs and to bring the nine-year-old with them.

When the mother explained her plight, the assistant manager asked with empathy, "Are you telling me that the reason your boys stole food is because you're hungry?"

With head down and eyes tightly shut to hold off the tears that threatened to flow, the mother barely uttered a tired, whispery, "Yes."

The assistant manager went to her purse and took out fifty dollars in cash. She then went to all the other store employees for additional money.

The employees generously gave and the assistant manager soon had enough money to put the family into a motel for the night and pay for their breakfast the next morning.

The manager then arranged for the family to be immediately placed at Sacred Heart House, an interim shelter for single mothers with children.

Today, that mother and her three children live in a duplex in Denver. The mother is working at a 7-11 store and her husband has joined them. They are a family once again and can now take care of their children's needs.

The only reason I found out about this story is that my wife was volunteering at the shelter that took in the mother and her three sons.

When my wife returned home that evening from working at the shelter she told me the story of what our employees had done.

Now, let's look at the story with some logic.

Stealing is wrong, isn't it?

It's in the policy manual. However, this is an unusual circumstance. I wonder how many of us would have done the same thing in the same circumstances. The assistant manager did not just react to the obvious. If she did, she would have called the police without listening to the mother.

Instead, this assistant manager with a heart did some digging for facts and discovered a way she could help – by doing something good for someone else.

If your organization acts with sincere compassion towards all customers, than you have truly created an organization of Quiet Heroes. Don't judge people. Help people. It's more fun running a business that way.

CHAPTER

6

Model Yourself After the Best

How do you instill high customer service standards in your employees?

One way is to convince your employees they can be Super Heroes.

Another way is to show your employees examples of great customer service (and bad customer service) from other companies in other industries.

When I was president of King Soopers Supermarkets, we had a long range planning meeting three days each year. The first year we put together the meeting, I told our executive committee that there would be only one agenda item at the meeting: Improving customer service.

We decided that one way to help our employees raise their standards of customer service was to get them to think outside the box. We told our employees that we wanted to model ourselves after the best customer service companies in the country.

It was not enough to be the best customer service supermarket in the Denver area. Several polls showed that customers rated us tops in service in our marketplace. The customer standards in the supermarket industry were so low that you could be the best supermarket with relatively poor service.

I told my employees to look at companies in other

industries, such as Nordstrom and the Ritz-Carlton Hotel. If our company could match their standard of service, then we could be really proud of ourselves.

Nordstrom is the department store chain famous for its customer service.

Nordstrom has an employee handbook that is 75 words long (yes, words, not pages). Included in the handbook are two rules:

Rule #1: Use good judgment at all times.

Rule #2: There are no more rules.

One often-told story is that Nordstrom gave one of its customers a refund on two used automobile tires. A customer told one of their clerks that he had purchased two tires at another Nordstrom store (out-of-state) and that he wanted his money back. The employees gave him his money back.

The amazing part of the story is that none of the Nordstrom stores sells tires.

I told this story to a group of our employees, emphasizing the exceptional service Nordstrom expects its employees to give.

About three weeks later I received a call from our mail room asking, "Don, are you expecting a tire?"

"No, I am not expecting a tire."

"Well, there is one here for you."

I went straight to the mail room and, sure enough, there was a beat-up old tire with an note attached to it from the employees of one of our stores.

The note said, "Don, we want you to know we were listening to you. Last week a woman came through the check stand and after we rang up the groceries, she didn't have enough money to pay for them. We asked if she had anything she could sell us.

"She said, 'Yes, I have three used automobile tires,' so we gave her $5 for each tire.

"This one is yours. What do you want us to do with the other two?"

At least they were listening.

Here is another example of exceptional service from Nordstrom.

A woman returned a cocktail dress she had obviously worn. Nordstrom gave the woman her money back.

When Nordstrom cleaned the dress, they noticed that the woman had left a handkerchief in the pocket. Do you know what Nordstrom did? They laundered the handkerchief and mailed it back to the woman, telling her that she had inadvertently left it in the dress.

Think about it. Anyone's normal reaction would be that the woman might have been trying to take advantage of Nordstrom. But Nordstrom decided to take the long view.

Someday that same woman may have enough money to buy a good dress that she plans on keeping.

Where do you think she will go to make that purchase?

These examples may prove a bit irritating for many readers. Nordstrom obviously could not stay in business if it let all its customers cheat the stores.

But the point is that most of Nordstrom's customers, most of my customers, most of your customers are honest. To let a few bad people get away with a few bad deeds will not hurt profits significantly. To assign bad motives to all your customers because of a few bad incidents can destroy your company.

That is why we do not question customers who return merchandise. And that is why we have to train our employees to ignore their suspicions in many cases and not to argue with the customer. Our business will grow if we let the customers win all the close calls.

Nordstrom sets a high bar for a retail operation. But there are other companies that also exhibit great customer service. One of these companies is The Ritz-Carlton.

How The Ritz-Carlton handles service

The Ritz-Carlton hotel in Boston won the Malcolm Baldridge National Quality Award, which is awarded to the very best companies in the country.

During one of my business trips out east, I decided to go stay there to see if the hotel lived up to its claims and other's accolades. Much to my surprise, the experience was even better than I imagined.

I happened to overhear a guest tell the concierge that the mattress they were sleeping on was a problem. She explained that her husband was a large man in stature and she was small, and well, the mattress sunk to one side.

The woman told how, every time she moved, she rolled over to her husband's side. It is fortunate that her husband blocked her fall, even though he was the reason she was rolling to his side.

The concierge (even though taking care of faulty mattresses was not part of his job description) responded by telling the couple that the hotel would fix the situation right away. He promised that someone would change the mattress before the couple returned from their shopping trip.

Every employee at The Ritz-Carlton is empowered to take care of a problem. They give their employees the flexibility to take care of a guest concern, up to a $2,000 make-good expense.

One morning, during our stay at the hotel, a guest was talking to his wife about the dinner they ate the night before in the hotel dining room. The husband was disappointed, feeling that the meal was not up to par. The maid, who was busy changing the linens, overheard the conversation. She immediately went to the phone, called the hotel manager and had the restaurant charge removed from the couple's hotel bill. The day manager took care of it based on the conversation with the maid, knowing that staff had the authority to make that kind of a request on behalf of a guest.

The maid did not have to check with a supervisor higher up on the employee food chain.

She had the power and she used it.

The customer benefited and the employee felt powerful.

Nordstrom and Ritz-Carlton offer consistently good customer service. But there are many other companies that provide examples of how to treat the customer.

Capital Grill is a restaurant in Denver. When you make a reservation they ask if you are celebrating a special occasion and if there is anything extra you would like while you are at the restaurant. When we go there for dinner, they treat us like guests, not customers. Recently, a guest pulled up in front for their free valet parking and told the parking attendant not to take the car too far because it was low on gas. Guess what – the attendant put gas in the car for the customer.

Not so great customer service

I look hard for instances of great customer service because most companies and most industries are so poor in meeting the ordinary needs of their customers. When I receive mediocre or poor performance, I let the company know they are disappointing me.

Consider my experience with Acura cars.

Over the years, our family purchased seven Acura automobiles from the same dealership.

We liked the cars and overlooked the fact that our service appointments took far longer than we expected. Often, the wait was one week or more for a service appointment. When the car was finally taken in, the waits for servicing or repairs was often very long. I had to perfect the art of "loaner car begging" to obtain some transportation when the service department finally took our car in for service.

One winter I ordered four new snow tires for my Acura from the service department.

Shortly after the new tires were installed, my wife and I were driving back from the mountains going 70 miles an hour when the right front tire "pulled" apart like a blowout.

Once we returned home, I took both the car and the bad tire back to the service department.

I told the service department about how my wife and I were driving (on new tires) when a tire blew apart. The service department only wanted to replace the tire that pulled apart. I did not want to keep the other three tires which were bought at the same time.

Would you?

Two weeks later the service department finally contacted me. A clerk in the service department answered my question of what the dealer was willing to do.

This clerk said they "wouldn't do anything this time but they would be willing to give me credit the next time I buy a new car."

I should not have to tell you that I have never bought another Acura.

Think about it.

Through the years, we spent about $210,000 on our seven Acuras. We endured long waits at the service department and a tire blowout and we were still willing to continue as customers.

The sad part about this story is that many other car dealerships maintain the same cavalier attitude toward their customers.

And the automobile industry is not alone in this attitude.

If you really want to get my blood boiling, just talk to me about insurance companies.

I had State Farm Insurance for about 20 years and with six kids in our family, I carried the insurance on the kids' cars as well as our own. I was averaging $7,000 a year on insurance for all of our family cars as well as my home.

In 1993, after driving for 43 years without ever having an accident or a moving violation (St. Christopher was a frequent passenger of mine), I was driving with my wife on I-70, going west out of the Eisenhower tunnel on a clear sunny day. It had snowed the day before, but the roads were clear.

As I moved at 70 mph, I looked up ahead and saw what appeared to be a glob of black snow.

As I got closer, my wife said, "That looks like a rock."

Sure of myself, I replied in a patient tone, "No, it's only black snow."

It was a rock.

You never want to drive over a rock that you had just identified as a glob of snow with your wife sitting in the car telling you that the snow sure looks like a rock to her.

Our insurance paid $4,100 to fix the car.

One month later, I received notification that my insurance rates were about to go up substantially.

I called my insurance agent and asked why.

He said, "Because you had an accident."

I replied, "I know that, but did anybody check my record? There were no accidents, no tickets, no claims for over 20 years."

He responded, "Even if the president of State Farm has an accident, his rates go up."

"That's too bad for your president, because I'm changing companies and maybe your president would want to change with me."

Think about it.

$7,000 a year, multiplied by 20 years of purchasing insurance without many claims … is $140,000.

That is what was lost to the company I was leaving because they apparently did not review files on a case-by-case basis. As a result, I switched to Farmer's

Insurance and did so at the same rate I had with State Farm Insurance before my one accident.

Now, I don't know if Farmer's Insurance is any better than my former company's product, because I have not had to file a claim testing their system. However, if I do file a claim and they raise my rates, I'll be sure to switch again.

It's a pretty odd industry that goes out of its way to fire good customers.

Other industries seem to have the same attitude as car dealerships and insurance companies.

I've noticed that a lot of airline companies have recently filed for bankruptcy.

Maybe it's because the skies you fly are not so friendly.

Here is a perfect example of an industry that is truly anti-customer. Everything this industry does is against the customer base they serve.

Airlines now charge extra if your luggage weighs over fifty pounds.

If you need to change your ticket, the cost is $100.

On a recent business trip, I heard the airline captain making the usual announcements about landing – with one addition.

He said, "Make sure you clean up around your seat so the flight attendants do not have to."

I was in shock.

I suddenly felt as if I was back in grade school and had just been told to clean my desk before going home.

It's no wonder that consumers have the attitude we hold about this industry. This type of service from huge industries that show an obvious lack of caring for their customers forces this attitude on the public.

There are exceptions. JetBlue Airways has never lost money. JetBlue CEO David Neeleman said, "We've just kind of rethought the system and said, 'Let's treat our customers like customers.' Let's not treat them like they're trying to game the system or try and make rules to stop them. If you keep trying to beat down your customers, they eventually just feel they're not appreciated." Maybe that attitude is why JetBlue Airways has planes full of customers.

It's not like I'm alone in having these feelings about airlines, car dealers and insurance companies. Many of the transactions we are most anxious about – flying on an airplane, making an insurance claim, getting service on our cars, even eating in a restaurant – are filled with annoyances. If businesses would treat their customers with more respect and more care, then these transactions would not be sources of such dread.

Businesses that truly care about their customers, like Nordstrom, like The Ritz-Carlton hotels, create loyal customers and make money year after year. When a business really tries to have great customer service, almost every obstacle can be overcome.

For example, take the restaurant in downtown Denver that was located right in the middle of an improvement project. The city announced the closing of a bridge that cut off most of the direct traffic to the restaurant.

The street became a construction zone with hardhat workers and cars detoured to non-existent exits.

The restaurant owner had nightmarish visions of vacant tables and lost customers.

The restaurant started a radio and television

campaign, telling everyone that downtown is changing and that people need to change with it. Customers who fought the obstacles and visited the restaurant anyway were issued mock construction helmets by the restaurant staff.

Staff also gave the construction crew stickers to give to passersby telling them how to get to the restaurant.

Many businesses in the construction zone experienced large losses during the construction period. However, this restaurant's business rose 22% from the previous year.

When you are in business, you expect to encounter obstacles. The trick is to be aware of your customers' problems and to work with your customers to solve those problems and provide a great shopping experience.

When your company is dealing with customers, ask yourself the question, "Are we giving the same quality of service that The Ritz-Carlton hotel and Nordstrom would give?"

If not, it may be time to make some changes.

Trust Your Employees

I am a firm believer that the better we treat our employees, the better our employees will treat our customers.

Employees do not get up every morning asking, "Gee, what can I do today to mess up the company?" If our organization wants our employees to have a good attitude toward our customers, everyone on the management team must give employees the benefit of the doubt.

Of course an organization must have rules of conduct. Rules make it easy for everyone to know they are doing the right thing. When rules are easy to understand and sensible, everyone in the company should know what is expected.

The hard part is when somebody breaks the rules. Then you have to use a little judgment to find out why the rules were broken.

Take Mark, for example.

One day, I got a call from a manager who said, "I am going to step two on an employee."

This meant that under our union contract a proposed firing was being taken to arbitration.

The employee was Mark.

"How come?"

"The employee's absentee record and late attendance

have gone far enough. So we fired him."

"Okay. I'll be there to attend the step two proceedings."

Here is some background. Mark was a nineteen-year-old without much of a formal education. While many young adults have a choice of work or school, Mark had no choice – it would have to be work.

When Mark returned late from his break one night – with no apology for being late – he went to his workstation.

The head clerk said, "Mark, you do that again and you'll be fired, do you understand?"

"Okay," mumbled Mark.

The next night Mark returned from his break ten minutes late again. The head clerk was past simmering.

He was boiling.

The head clerk fired Mark, just as he had promised.

We scheduled a meeting that, in addition to Mark and me, included the union representative, the store manager, the assistant store manager and service department managers.

I began the meeting by asking the group, "Has anyone here asked Mark why he is absent so often or is frequently late? You have many notes in his file, but nowhere does it state why he has done these things, especially after being reprimanded."

Finally one of the managers spoke.

He said, "Don, he knows he is supposed to be here and not be late – after all, that's why we hired him."

"I know," I said. "But is it possible that this young man grew up in a home where the parents did not care if Mark was on time for school or even absent? Isn't it possible that Mark attended a school that never phoned the parents to ask the whereabouts of their child when a student was missing or late?"

The manager whispered, "Yes, that's possible."

"Let's follow this thought through to completion," I added. "Mark comes to work for our company and he is supposed to know that he needs to be at work on time and to not be absent unless ill."

The heads were nodding in unison. I continued. "I know it is logical for you to know that, but is it logical for Mark to know that?"

It was obvious from their silence that I had their attention and they were accepting my slant on the situation.

I asked, "Does anyone mind if we offer Mark his job back? Let's at least listen to his side of the story."

Enter Mark. He looked like the wrath of God – no socks, dusty shoes, unshaven and wearing a dirty t-shirt.

Speaking in a soft tone, Mark looked to his shoes instead of looking at the people in the room. He explained that the reason he was late so often was that he was trying to get his mother and father together. They had been separated for some time and he was trying to get them to attend a family picnic.

Mark continued to explain that the second night he showed up late he did so because he found his father. He was so emotional he had lost track of time on both nights.

I told Mark how important he was to the store. I gave Mark a forty-five minute talk on the importance of his job. I asked him if he could replace this job if we fired him. He told us, "Probably not."

I had an idea.

I asked Mark if he would buy a watch if we agreed to give him his job back. "Yes," he said.

This was the first time all night that he stood up straight.

So, we put Mark back to work.

After Mark left the meeting, I told the management group, "You can always fire him. His file is full. Let's wait and see what happens."

Six months later, to the day of the meeting, I was walking though the cafeteria when a person stopped me and said, "Hey, remember me?"

I looked at him.

His eyes were familiar but I could not place him. Then, I asked him if he was Mark. He nodded, appreciating that I remembered him.

This Mark stood up straight and was dressed in a suit and tie. He told me he had been promoted – that he was here for checker training class.

I said, "That's great – have you ever been late again?"

He pointed to his watch and said, "No, I have my watch now. Isn't that great?"

I didn't know that Mark's situation would turn out like that, but it showed that sometimes people can surprise you if you give them a chance.

In addition, the process taught management how to handle situations the next time a Mark-like employee enters their lives.

There is always a reason for behavior.

Search for the reason and you may save the employee.

How to handle problem employees

I am often asked the question, "How do you create a climate designed to help drive success of your people?"

When an employee does something that's obviously wrong, I recommend that you do not chew him out or write him up.

Instead, ask your employee why he did what he did so that you can learn from his viewpoint. Then you can try to explain to the employee why you think his behavior was wrong and how he can modify the behavior to meet the needs of the company.

When I attend department head meetings where the subject of under-producing employees is discussed, some managers always talk about how to "write-up" employees to create a paper trail for firing.

I would ultimately ask one question – "Who in here is going to help the employee succeed?"

Who is willing to spend the time to help an employee? How can an employee find success if he or she is "written up" after a first misstep?

You can always fire an employee, but that ought to be the last resort, not the first action.

One day when entering one of my stores I was distracted by a sign that caught my attention.

It was located above the time clock. The sign read, "From now on, anyone who phones in sick must bring a doctor's excuse upon return." The sign was from "THE MANAGEMENT."

I asked the assistant, "Do you mean everyone has to bring an excuse?"

His answer was an abrupt "Yep."

"Why?" I said.

"Absenteeism is high and we have to control it."

"Wow, it must really be bad."

"Yep, it sure is."

"You have about 120 employees in this store. About how many do you estimate are considered as an absenteeism problem – 8 or 9?" Rapidly (at least he knew his statistics), he said, "Oh no, not that many."

"Not that many? Then how many?"

"Three or four."

"Because of three or four people, you mean to tell me everyone has to bring a doctor's excuse?"

"Yep, got to."

"Why?

"Because the union says so – you have to treat everyone equal."

"But," I argued, "That's not treating everyone equally. If the 3 or 4 call in sick, they should have to bring a doctor's excuse.

"The others should not have to come up with a doctor's excuse unless they develop the same habit as the 3 or 4.

"*That* is how to treat people equally."

Learning from employees

As a district manager, I would frequently visit our stores to talk with employees for an inside view of what was happening on the job.

You would be surprised about what you can learn from employees on the front lines. I often showed up unannounced to visit our night crews, to try to find out our employees' true feelings.

During one of these visits, and at the end of a long night crew shift, the grocery manager had a meeting to inform the crew that we were all going out to breakfast. He then proceeded to tell the crew that they were "doing a good job," adding that since it was coming up to our busiest season – the holidays – he had an announcement.

"This year, around Christmas time, there will be NO vacations allowed for anyone."

Eyebrows and blood pressures went up simultaneously.

Can you imagine how that declaration made everyone feel? The anger permeated the entire crew – including those who did not even want to be off for the holidays.

After that statement, we all left for the breakfast meeting. As we rode in the manager's car I casually asked, "George, when do you like to go on vacation?"

"Oh, always in October, during hunting season. That is my perfect vacation time."

"I don't think anybody should be off during that time. After all, it is Halloween and we have quite a few displays to get ready. Frankly, I do not think you should be off."

George stuttered and stammered out, "What do you mean?"

While he was still a little off-balance, I added, "It's all right for you to be off when you want and it's not all right for someone else to be off when they want?

"Is that fair?"

As he quickly regained composure, the manager replied, "But what if everybody wants off the week before Christmas?"

Now was the time to make my point. "First of all, I agree that you can't let everybody off at that time. However, before you make an announcement like you made, wait and see how many employees actually ask for time off over Christmas. Then, if nobody does, it is a non-issue and you have not upset the crew. How many people can you reasonably let off that week?"

"Probably two."

"Okay."

Whispering, he said, "All right, but what if three want off?"

As if I knew what he was going to say, I responded, almost too quickly, saying, "Simple. Bring the three together and tell them your problem. You can't let all three off but you can let two off and see if the three crew members can work out an exchange with one another.

"At least the employees will know you are trying to help them and are not ignoring their requests. I am willing to bet it is worked out better by turning it over to the crew."

As it turned out, only one person wanted off that week. The moral of this story: Do not anticipate a problem that does not exist.

Giving employees the benefit of the doubt

From time to time, employees would request time off for a particular personal event such as an anniversary dinner or a graduation ceremony of a relative.

To these kinds of requests, management would just say, "No, the job is more important."

The job is more important – to management.

You can imagine how attitude sinks into the depths when employees are denied time off for special occasions. They will call in sick and attend the events anyway, just as I would do if management had done that to me.

One evening when I surveyed the warehouse, Joe, a forklift operator, came over to me asking if I might be able to help him with a problem his friend Bill was having.

"I'll try. What is it?"

"Bill's brother is graduating from high school on Friday night, and they won't let him off."

So, I asked the supervisor about Bill's request and the supervisor told me he was aware of it.

"Why aren't you granting him time off?"

He answered, "You know, Friday is our busiest night and we need everybody we can get. And besides," he continued, "Bill's selection rate is horrible."

"What's that got to do with letting him off? Does he have a brother?"

The supervisor nodded, "Yes."

"Is the brother graduating on Friday night?"

The supervisor said, "Yes."

Then I knew that the supervisor is going to need more than a little help to get back on the right management track.

"So, let him off," I said.

He thought for a moment, scratched his head and (by this time I hoped I was getting somewhere) said, "But his selection rate is one of the lowest…"

To which I responded, "That's not a good enough reason for not letting him have time off. His low productivity is your fault. You should train him to get his production level up. And, in the meantime, let him off on Friday night. He's going to call in sick anyway, isn't he?"

Can stealing be forgiven?

Stealing by employees in most companies, including ours, results in the immediate termination of the employee or employees involved. However, when one of our employees was accused of stealing, we suspended the accused employees until each case was thoroughly investigated to make sure our company was being fair.

Here's why:

One Christmas, when I was a district manager, I got to know a female meat cutter who had been through a divorce and was left with the sole responsibility of raising her three children. She had worked for our store for over twenty-two years.

Days away from Christmas Eve, the woman left her shift and took home three pairs of winter gloves to give to her children as gifts because she was "strapped." She was suspended for further investigation.

The president of the company, Ray Rose, stopped by and asked me how it was going. I told him I didn't think we had a choice. She should be fired.

He pointed out that this employee had worked for us a long time and had a clean record. He pointed out that the employee was under a lot of pressure and had made a mistake that a lot of other people might make.

He said, "You can still terminate her, but nothing says you can't re-hire her, does it?" So, we terminated her for one day and rehired her in our meat processing plant the next day. She is still working for us.

I have thought about that incident for years. We all make mistakes and it would have been a shame for her to lose her job for one error in judgment under extreme pressure.

Our president's words made a powerful impression on me. He showed great leadership and was one of my best teachers on how to help employees succeed by showing compassion.

CHAPTER

8

Creating Satisfied Employees

The first step you can take as a manager or owner toward having satisfied customers is to have satisfied employees.

Treat all your employees with dignity and remember that each employee is an individual, with different needs and aspirations.

I learned that lesson in 1972, when I was director of distribution for King Soopers. In that capacity, I had four warehouses and a transportation department under my direction. As you can imagine, we were always searching for quality supervisors with work experience in warehouse situations.

One day, one of our supervisors told me about Tony. Tony was a truck driver. I was surprised to learn that not only was Tony a college graduate, but he had also been a former schoolteacher and had a master's degree.

I invited Tony to come in to my office. "Tony," I said, "Why, with that background, are you driving a truck?"

"I like driving a truck," he replied.

I asked him if he would ever consider a job in management. Tony paused, then said he would think about it.

Tony agreed to try a supervisor position for a few weeks and see how it worked for him. I hoped the new job would grow on him and he would start to like his new career track.

After three weeks, Tony came in to see me. He said that he appreciated the opportunity to become a manager, but he would rather drive a truck.

It has been twenty-five years. Tony is still driving a truck. Tony and his wife have five children and they have all graduated from college on the salary that Tony earned from the career he loves – driving a truck.

Now here is the point of my story. No one will ever convince me that I am any happier than Tony is, even though our jobs and our salary levels were vastly different. Tony is doing what he wants and I'm doing what I want. We are both still achieving a life wish. The life wish differs from person to person.

How to handle a bad boss

I think that one of the jobs of the president of a company is to make all the employees feel comfortable in their jobs. To that end, I held regular meetings with employees to answer their questions and reinforce company policies.

One day, during one of my programs, an audience participant said aloud, "I think what you're saying about customer service is great. But I cannot use what you say because I have a bad boss."

When you have a bad boss – and all of us have had one from time to time – the best thing you can do is to help make that boss successful so he gets promoted, paving the way for you to get a new boss. Make sure you provide your boss with honest feedback when he asks a question. And if you don't agree with a decision your boss makes, try to cooperate and hope for a better result the next time around.

Promote your boss and you win the prize – a new and hopefully better model than your former boss.

Personalized service

In a large company, it is crucial to have common goals. One of our most important goals was to treat every customer with dignity and respect. During training, we impressed upon the employees that they should make an effort to always use the customer's name whenever possible.

To use the customer's name, you must first obtain it.

"Squuuuze me," "Ma'am" or "Sir" does not work.

You need to listen for customer's names and then use them in conversation to personalize a transaction.

There is always a way to obtain a customer's name.

For example, whenever a customer writes out a check, the name will be available. Over the years, I have found that nothing is more impressive to anyone than using a person's name when completing a sales or service function. Customers like to hear their names.

The interaction becomes personal and establishes a relationship.

Besides making customers feel better, communicating with them on a personal basis was also good for our business.

We monitored our average customer count and found that it averaged 20,000 customers per week per store. We estimated that a startling sales increase could happen if that average sale increased by only fifty cents, adding $10,000 per week to sales.

We asked our checkout clerks to ask customers if they found everything.

If the customer said "No," another staff member would be sent to get the item not located. Our customers appreciated the personal service, which had the added benefit of improving our bottom line.

The importance of fixing problems

When I was director of distribution, I visited our locations to talk with employees and get to know them as people – outside the job.

I wanted to learn more about how our people do their jobs and what we could do to make it easier for them to accomplish what we asked of them.

One day I had a conversation with one of our truck drivers while he sat in the cab of his truck.

Noticing that his seat had a spring protruding directly through the fabric, I asked, "Bob, why don't you get that fixed or replaced?"

With an edge of disgust in his voice, Bob responded, "I keep asking them and they just keep putting it off."

To this I asked, "How long has this been going on?"

He shrugged and responded, "Sixteen months."

I thought, "Wow, we must really be busy with a backlog of work to do if it takes this long to fix a seat spring."

After this conversation, I went right to our transportation manager to ask about Bob's truck.

He said, "Yeah, Bob is always complaining."

Ignoring his comment, I said, "Just replace the seat,

will you?"

With attitude, he barked, "It'll cost $150."

"So?"

"And besides, Bob has a lot of unnecessary overtime."

"What's that got to do with the seat?" I asked.

I told the transportation manager to fix the seat.

Now, can you guess what happened after the seat was fixed?

Bob's unnecessary overtime went away.

Sometimes there are managers who want to "get even" with workers who seem to cause them problems. I would argue that it is actually management's fault for their workers' attitudes. Bob had an unanswered, legitimate complaint that management was obviously ignoring. His manager's attitude was, "It's always the worker's fault."

As managers and leaders, we need to look at ourselves as the "mirror" of our employee's behavior.

The only factor that makes all the difference is attitude. Treat others with respect and they will do the same.

Making customers happy

Bad attitude leaves a bad mark.

We wanted to find a way to quickly handle the small problems that sometimes come up while shopping. We all know that when customers have a bad experience, they leave the store mad. Those angry customers now can't wait to tell someone about their bad experiences. Typically, in these situations, management has no clue as to what has transpired. The fact is that a customer left the store angry.

That is not acceptable.

Each angry customer is like a billboard advertising what we are doing wrong. That can't be good for business.

We came up with a remedy – an idea that not only proved to be unique but also had long-reaching implications.

We provided each employee with a small, easy-to-carry coupon book. Employees were taught to use the coupon book with customers who needed an instant apology for a bad shopping experience.

Each coupon was redeemable for either a free video rental or a half-gallon of ice cream. We made sure every employee had a coupon book. This directive included all our employees – from the front line staff to the warehousemen and truck drivers.

Everyone was to carry and use this book – including managers.

Here was our plan.

We felt that with that as many employees as were in our organization – 15,000 – there was an increased likelihood that negative encounters would be intercepted immediately.

We would be able to appease angry shoppers. Poor customer service would be replaced with positive attention to the matter with an immediate effort of making it better. The customer would feel important. The best part of the program was that all of our employees, from front-line to transportation, were invested in a program that served our customer.

We had the key to a good recovery of a delicate situation…and our employees were empowered by being "in charge" of correcting the situation.

Of course, if whatever happened to the customer was so bad that could not easily be appeased with a coupon for ice cream or a movie, the employee was instructed to fill out a form for management, who were instructed to follow up quickly.

But by quickly lessening our customers' anger, we were able to foster loyalty and mutual respect instead of hurt feelings and lost business.

Part III
Management

CHAPTER
9

Working With the Union

Want to strike (yes, "strike") fear into a meeting of managers? Whisper the work "union," and conversation stops, people look around and a hesitant hush descends over the room.

Many managers fear and distrust unions and their business agents.

However, the unions represent our employees. Our employees are our company. We have to get along with the unions or our company will suffer.

Now, I often disagreed with the unions' business agents. We had plenty of disputes about wages or work conditions. But I always found our company ran far more smoothly when the union and management teams respected each other and worked together for the benefit of the employees and the company.

That's where Bill Jenkins came in.

When I was a district manager, I wanted to improve our relationship with the unions. I asked each of the store managers to take their business agents to lunch at least once a quarter to listen to concerns. After a lengthy discussion, all nine store managers said, "That's fine. However, you can't possibly include Bill Jenkins."

Bill Jenkins had developed quite a reputation as a pushy business agent who encouraged employees to file frivolous grievances. My managers proceeded to tell me about the evils of Bill Jenkins, adding, "No one can deal with him."

My response: "Let's wait until I meet with him and then we'll talk about this again."

I called Bill to schedule a lunch with him, without stating the purpose of the meeting.

I had not yet met with Bill. But I already disliked him.

My managers helped to form my opinion without my ever having met Bill. Logic told me I should know better. But I couldn't help wondering if my managers were right and I was crazy to meet with Bill Jenkins.

Bill and I met for lunch. That lunch changed my view of unions and business agents forever. It turned out that Bill Jenkins was a World War II veteran who had been honored as a Purple Heart recipient.

We talked for several hours. I was disappointed when Bill finished his fascinating war stories.

Then I changed topics: "What problems do my managers cause you?"

Bill thought for a while and then replied, "There are two or three managers who give me nothing but grief."

Bill told me how the managers reacted to every grievance – how they would not settle in step two, when a union dispute is the subject of a meeting.

Bill told me that the managers kept taking their grievance to arbitration. Bill said, "That's costly and it creates poor morale." He emphasized that most disputes could be settled early and fairly.

"From now on," I said, "If you feel you're not getting a 'fair shake' on any grievance, don't hesitate to call me. Now, I'm not saying I'm going to agree with you, but I'll listen and be fair. Deal?"

"Okay," Bill agreed.

At my next managers' meeting, I told the managers to stop trying to get even with Bill. I knew they were taking the grievances further because they didn't like Bill, not necessarily because it was always the right course of action. "I understand that you think Bill is not likeable. But, likeable or not, you will have to learn to manage Bill."

From that day on, I made sure that in my district the unions and their agents were treated with respect. The result: In our district very few grievances went past step two and went to arbitration. When an issue came up with Bill Jenkins, I gave in on some issues and Bill gave in on some issues.

Isn't that the way union and management should behave?

I remember one incident when we tried to fire an employee for theft. This evidence on the theft charge was not very solid.

This particular employee also had drug problems. Although we had documented that we did everything we could do to turn him into a good, productive employee, there was evidence that he could not shake his drug problem.

We were in arbitration. From my experience, I wasn't sure we could win this at arbitration. But I hoped to resolve the matter in a way that would not harm the employee or the company. I asked Bill Jenkins to step out of the meeting for a moment.

In a quiet corner, I told Bill, "Look, this guy is a problem, not only for us, but he represents a problem for you, too. Why don't you go in and tell him that we will not press charges if he resigns?"

Bill did it.

The union business agent, whom none of my managers could get along with, became my ally in solving difficult issues for the company and its employees. In fact, fifteen years later, when I became president, Bill Jenkins was one of the first people who called to personally congratulate me.

Good people can disagree on an issue. The key is to treat the employees and unions with respect and any problems can usually be solved without hard feelings.

Raising productivity despite a union strike

While I was director of distribution, I was in charge of three warehouses along with the related transportation to support those warehouses.

When I first arrived, overall productivity was at an all-time low. Morale was also at an all-time low. The condition of the facility was horrible.

Our employees demonstrated that although they were slow to do their jobs, they were gifted with rapid writing skills. The employees were members of the Teamsters union and would write grievances faster than we could review them.

Every day, when I arrived at work, I noticed a new stack of grievances on the manager's desk. I started to ask some questions of my management team.

"Why are there so many grievances?"

One manager growled an answer, "Those guys are a bunch of sorry losers."

Isn't that telling? I knew I had a lot of work to do.

I love the way situations can generate ideas if you let them. So, I started walking this grocery warehouse facility over the next month. I walked all three shifts and got to know every employee so I could understand each person better... and most importantly, get a handle on what was so upsetting in the workplace.

I know that people do not just write grievances because they are in need of a hobby – there is always a substantial reason.

The reason in this situation was clear – the employees were angry with us for the way we were treating them. They perceived us to be the enemy.

What do you do when you encounter the enemy?

You fight.

In our workplace, productivity was based on a selection rate. This selection rate refers to the number of cases per hour an employee could select from the warehouse to fill an order. Each order is different and based on each individual store's needs and requests.

The merchandise cases were a myriad of sizes and shapes. Some employees were better at selection than others. When I started as director of distribution, our productivity was at an all-time low: a selection rate of 115 cases per hour. The industry rate for selection was 150 cases per hour. We made that our goal. We had some catching up to do.

Upon reviewing the situation, I decided that the fault of the lower productivity was not the fault of the employees. It was the fault of management. My managers had a hard time accepting my theory because, as they said, "We are not the ones selecting cases!"

But I thought that the employees just needed encouragement, positive feedback and some new work rules to improve their selection rate.

We started to implement management changes, getting the work force to endorse a new "team" concept. But shortly, a stumbling block appeared. We went into negotiations with the Teamsters for a new labor agreement.

These negotiations did not just involve us – they included all the supermarket chains in our area. It was a global negotiation, meaning that a strike against one would be a strike against all of us.

After negotiations failed, the Teamsters went on strike for 17 days.

We had to pitch in to do the physical work. During the strike, management selected orders, made deliveries to the stores and, in the process, learned how hard it is to run a good warehouse and transportation system. The strike actually made our managers pull together and really understand what our workers faced every day.

It was not surprising that after this, our management was far more appreciative of our work force. We also learned how easy it is to make mistakes. The work force had to clean up our mistakes for many weeks after the strike!

I remember one situation when I dispatched an empty trailer 70 miles south of our store location.

The driver said, "I thought the truck felt light when I arrived at the dock."

Oh, well. I guess that showed our managers that I was human and just as likely to make a mistake as anyone.

Because we had begun to develop such a good relationship with our employees before the strike started, the union steward assured me that he would keep some of the "rabble-rousers" separated at the store's picket lines as a means of lessening problems.

In the 17 days of that strike, we never once had to get a restraining order to keep our employees in line. But our competition did have to rely on restraining orders.

The strike settled on a Friday. We needed to move on to business as usual, and do so very quickly. We needed to have our workers come back to work on the following Saturday and Sunday. That would require paying time and a half for the weekend work.

Our competition decided there was no way they were going to bring back their workers and pay them time and a half after they had been on strike.

We requested that all of our workers come in that Friday afternoon. We gathered in the cafeteria that featured a big sign, reading, "WELCOME BACK."

At the meeting, we said, "We know you have been on the picket line and away from your families a lot, but we would like you to work both Saturday and Sunday to get us back up to speed."

We admitted that management couldn't possibly do the job that our employees could do and our stores were in a "world of hurt."

And we added, "Don't bring your lunch, we'll feed you."

Feed them we did.

Our delicatessen catered all three shifts both days.

On the Sunday following the strike, one of the workers was so impressed by our actions that he called a local television station to report what we were doing.

I received a call from the television station asking if they could do an interview, filming me at our warehouse.

The television reporter asked me, "Why are you doing this, feeding the strikers? Aren't you angry? After all, these guys were on strike."

I responded, "The strikers are our employees. Our employees have been on the picket line for 17 days and away from their families. Now, they are giving up Saturday and Sunday to help us get back in full business. It's the right thing to do."

The story was the lead news item headlined on television that night.

Everyone was talking about it.

You can't buy that kind of advertising.

Before the strike, our business was ahead 17% over the previous year. After the strike, we were up 27%.

And as far as grievances and productivity issues – after we implemented all our new procedures, grievances were nonexistent and productivity was at an all-time high at 172 cases per hour (a 50% improvement and much higher than the average). Our competition had a hard time recovering from the ill feelings they attributed to the strike. They blamed the strike for their shortfalls and their employees blamed them.

In a strike situation, there are always a few individuals who use the opportunity as an excuse to damage company property. We had an incident and we filed charges.

Three of our employees were to appear in court

shortly after the strike. Those three individuals were considered troublemakers.

But those same troublemakers were also natural leaders among the work force. The employees rallied behind them.

The day before the trio was scheduled to appear in court, my boss suggested to me that we drop the charges on those three individuals. I thought he was crazy because this was a great opportunity to get rid of three troublemakers. But my boss said they were also leaders to the rest of the work force and this was an opportunity to bring them back as allies if handled properly.

He suggested I call them in my office one at a time and tell them we were going to drop the charges on the condition that they stop filing unnecessary grievances and help us run the warehouse.

They agreed, and we never had another problem with our warehouse employees. In fact, those three employees are still working in the warehouse, some twenty-three years later.

It would have been easy to punish the employees and try to set an example with our actions. My boss taught me a valuable lesson that helped me handle similar situations in the future. People make our business, and when we treat them with care and respect, our business will soar.

A second look at a difficult situation

Employees always seem to know about everyone's business at work. And even when the situation involves only one employee, it can affect everyone in the department.

I got a call from a retired union steward who had worked for us some years back.

She asked me to look into a situation at one of our stores where a head clerk was fired for stealing. Being caught stealing usually meant termination. However, this steward felt the individual in question was "set up" by security. The accused employee had been with us for twenty-one years and was going through a divorce made worse by financial problems.

I promised to look into it.

I found that security had placed a billfold with money in it at this employee's workstation. The employee took the money and left the billfold. He was put on suspension pending further investigation.

The store's employees sent me a petition defending their co-worker. They claimed we had set the employee up and we were unfair. They said he was a great employee. So much for confidentiality.

Wanting to be unbiased, I had the district manager look into the situation as well. The district manager still thought the man should be fired.

The easiest course for me to take would have been to enforce the firing of the employee. After all, we can't afford to have dishonest employees.

But the more I thought about the situation, the clearer it became that we had set the man up and now he was under the cloud we had created.

I decided to have the employee returned to work. Further, I said to pay him from the day he left work.

"We are admitting we made a mistake and he shouldn't have to pay for that."

The employee grapevine saw my decision as one of compassion, not of weakness. That attitude spread throughout the store and helped to improve the relationship between employees and management there.

Are you helping customers or stacking apples?

I liked and respected our employees. But, like most companies, we had some employees who actually hated their jobs. Just think how that must feel. Every day, employees who dread their workdays come to work with the words "I hate my job" imprinted on their foreheads.

These employees have to change their attitude or find another career.

One day, when I was making the rounds at one of our stores, I passed the produce department where a young man, about 17 years old, was stacking apples. I nodded and asked, "How's it going?"

He barked, "TERRIBLE!"

I asked, "Terrible, why terrible?"

"I keep stacking the apples and customers keep coming by and taking them off. So I need to start over and stack them all over again."

Ah, I said to myself, now I know the problem. This employee thinks his job is stacking apples and he is irritated that customers who buy apples are making him do the same job over and over again.

Customers keep interfering with his work task, as this young clerk sees it. Consequently, he has to keep starting over. Customers pick apples and he restacks them.

The fact that by stacking apples he is enticing customers to buy the apples did not enter into this young man's thinking process. I wanted to impress upon him that his stacking apples helped us obtain our goal of selling merchandise to customers.

Didn't anyone ever explain to him that his job was to sell apples? And if he was always stacking them up again, he must be doing a pretty good job.

I asked him, "How do you like working here?"

He said, "I hate it."

With eyebrows raised to the ceiling, I asked, "So, why are you doing this?" He shrugged his shoulders and responded in a lackadaisical manner, "I need the money."

Really? That was sad.

"I agree," I said. "We all need money. However," I added, "If the ONLY reason you are doing this job is for the money, then you need to stop, get out, quit and do something you really like."

I don't think he expected to hear that from his district manager.

"What? Huh?" and then, "Maybe you're right."

We had a long discussion then, not about stacking apples but about how to find what can make you happy in life. He has since moved on to another career, but he keeps in touch occasionally to let me know how he's doing.

Too many people spend their whole lives in the pursuit of money regardless of personal happiness. I know you can do both – earn a living while doing a job you enjoy. Life's too short to do anything else.

CHAPTER

10

Recognition and Reward

Whether you are working with customers, employees or managers, the same principles apply. According to behavioral experts, behavior is modifiable with rewards and recognition.

If you reward good behavior, you will see more and more of it. Ignore bad behavior and it should extinguish itself.

Most people perform better when their accomplishments are acknowledged. All of us know at least one workplace with a reputation for punishing the mistakes people make and ignoring the good work they do because it is expected.

I wanted the type of work environment that applauds employee effort and helps employees who want to move ahead.

My experience has always been that everyone who works in our organization, from the newly hired grocery bagger to the company president, is searching every day for a kind word and a pat on the back. Customers who come to our supermarkets are also searching for good feelings as well as food for the pantry.

Reward the people who provide front-line services and they will serve your customers better. It sounds so simple, and it works!

Focus on improvement, rather than volume

I learned a lot about human motivation when I first became district manager. When you are the new kid on the block, you are assigned some of the worst performing stores. I knew it would be an interesting challenge to try to get the stores up to par.

I invited the nine store managers who would report to me to lunch and a get-acquainted meeting.

After lunch, we casually discussed work-related issues. Interestingly, all my managers held the same perception about me and about the job. Each of them felt they were more qualified than I was and each had wanted the position of district manager.

Each one had been passed over.

And there I sat in front of them all.

I addressed the group.

"I know that some of you probably think you should have been promoted over me, and some of you might be right.

"However, I didn't do this.

"Someone in charge put me here.

"So, what I would like to hear from you is what you would like me to do as a district manager and also what can I do to help you become better store managers."

I concluded the conversation by telling them, "This is a closed session that will remain private among all of us. I promise the conversation will not leave this room."

It did not take long before the group began to unload. What they complained about most bitterly was lack of recognition. To the company, these were poor performing stores. To the store managers, they were doing their best to improve performance at stores that had disadvantages like small size, impoverished neighborhoods or older facilities. They said that no one in senior management recognized their stores when they had did well, or acknowledged the effort and achievement when a department in one of their stores had record sales.

"Heck," said one manager, "I had a record last week. No one even noticed.

"In fact," he continued, "I told one of the district managers and he said, 'That's nothing - did you hear what store #36 did?'"

I sympathized with the store manager. "That doesn't make your record anything less. Store 36 is in a neighborhood that should be doing that kind of volume. In fact, considering your location and size, I would argue that your record is probably better than store 36."

I continued, "Look, you guys, you can never be number one in volume because of your size and location, but you still make a tremendous contribution to our bottom line. And you can be the most improved store by ranking number one in the category of percent increase in sales.

"You can also be number one in the category of the most improved in productivity. It is impossible for all 70 stores to be number one in volume. But it is not impossible for your store to be the most improved in percent increases."

As a manager, you should measure and reward stores on how much they improve.

Everybody can improve.

If you focus on improvement rather than gross sales,

goals are attainable. Employees can see that the fruits of their efforts will be recognized.

We began an effort in my district to reward store managers for their sales increases over set periods of time. When a store manager met or exceeded the goal, he or she was recognized publicly by the company, as well as rewarded financially.

I never gave much credit when some supervisor said that he was 10 points above company average or 10 points below the company average. What does that mean?

If we have 70 stores, 35 of them will be above average and 35 will be below average. I do not care how you slice it – the results are the same. Averages are averages.

But percentage improvements can be measured and show real changes.

Setting a good tone for an organization

As company president, I knew that my behavior would set the tone for the rest of the company. I always enjoyed meeting employees and getting to know them. When I asked how things were, they told me. When I asked about family members, I was sincere.

It made a difference.

I have always felt that recognition of events is an important way to engage others and build relationships. Birthdays and anniversaries are important to people, so I tried to acknowledge them with a card. In addition, I asked the store managers to notify me of a serious illness or death in the family for any of their employees. In those cases, I would send a letter. I felt it was important enough to not just send a general note, but to be specific.

After all, the circumstance is important to the employee and it is a sincere way to show interest and concern.

A "letter to the editor" published in the *Denver Post* some years ago read:

"This past week, our dear friends lost their 21-year-old son from diabetic complications. In the midst of this pain and sorrow came many gestures of support and kindness.

"One of these gestures of compassion came unexpectedly from King Soopers, a giant in the food business. The folks at this giant demonstrated that 'big' does not necessarily mean 'cold.' The management of this food chain did not forget its own.

"This young man had worked for the chain less than a year, but the company treated his grieving family as if he had worked there forever.

"They sent tray after tray of food without fanfare to a very appreciative family that welcomed literally hundreds into their home as they accepted so many heartfelt condolences. They would never have been able to offer all those people the needed refreshments without this chain's loving and sensitive support.

"They did not have to do that. The president sent a sympathy letter. He did not have to do that. This is not a commercial for this chain. We did not have to do this. However, we thought that such a compassionate expression on the part of a big business like this chain should be shared with the Denver community. What they did, they did so quietly."

We did not send the food to receive the press coverage. But I always felt that good deeds often are rewarded in unexpected ways.

The importance of employee meetings

In order to motivate people, you have to communicate with them. I tried to do this in several ways.

I had individual contacts with many employees, and I always had an open door policy for all our employees. We had group meetings for management and smaller meetings for senior management.

But I also felt it was important to have group meetings with all our employees.

When I was president, we would have a quarterly meeting with twenty-five percent of all of our employees. This meeting was mandatory and was always held in a rented auditorium to accommodate large numbers of employees comfortably.

The purpose of this meeting was to discuss our sales and profits for the previous quarter. Before the meeting was over, we revealed our goals for the next quarter, giving people something tangible to work for.

We used motivation and frequent rewards to obtain the behavior we wanted. Sometime during each of the mandatory meetings, we announced a short break. During that break, employees were asked to take a moment to list one or two questions they would like to have answered by those in management.

Getting people to take that action – listing a question or complaint – was like getting people to volunteer for a root canal at the dentist. Employees would wait to see if someone else would do it and usually there were very few questions.

We decided we had to reward the behavior we

wanted. Each person who turned in a question, comment or complaint received a ticket that was entered into a drawing for a prize to be awarded that day.

The prize was a twenty-five dollar gift certificate from one of our stores. We drew four certificates at each meeting. Before the drawing for the certificate, we could count the number of responses to our request on one hand.

After the announcement of the reward, we saw the number of responses rise to where we wanted to see it. It was a great way to encourage employees to give us the feedback we wanted to hear. Employees quickly understood that we wanted better conditions for them, and that we would make changes based on their suggestions.

Our employees now felt that they had an "investment" in what management would work on to improve conditions for staff and for customers.

In these same quarterly meetings, we also acknowledged employees who had performed outstanding service the previous quarter by bringing them onstage, congratulating them and presenting them with a gift – all in front of their co-workers.

Let's do the math.

At a rate of 25% of the 15,000 employees in our organization, this activity affected 3,750 employees each quarter. To meet with that many employees, we had to have eight meetings per quarter, with approximately 500 employees attending each meeting. It was a demanding schedule, but we felt it was worth it.

By holding these meetings and encouraging employee participation, we felt as though our employees became more connected to the goals and aspirations of the organization. Our employees also saw that we cared about them and wanted to hear their opinions.

Performance counts, not credentials

One day a store checker came into my office and said he wanted to schedule a meeting. The clerk wanted to know what we had in store for him for his future.

"What do you mean?"

"Well, I am a college graduate and I'm just a checker. I look up and down the checkout stand area and I see other checkers there who do not have college degrees. However, I make the same pay they do. I think I am better than that because I have a college degree."

"Really?" I asked, dangling a report. "Would you like me to read you a part of an employee evaluation that your store manager wrote about you? Before you came in for your meeting, I asked your boss to tell me about you."

He quickly responded, "Okay, what did he say?"

"He said that you are a good worker who is never late or absent. He said that you are a good checker but that you do not have much ambition."

I waited for the next move – his.

"Well, you know," he said, "I don't report directly to that manager, so he really doesn't know what I do."

"I understand. But, if you are as good as you say you are, don't you think that your boss would tell the store manager about you?"

I said, "I'll tell you what. I want you to go back to your store and tell your service department manager that you want him to assign you to the courtesy clerk who is a problem to the service department. Add that if they do this, you will help make them successful.

"When you do that, do you think that will make them notice you?

"You see," I continued, "You not only have to be a good checkout clerk to get ahead in your job. We have 1500 checkers. You must be the BEST and your boss has to think so too.

"Do everything in the store that no one else wants to do, like cleaning up the lounge during your break and helping new employees feel welcome. Help under-producers become productive.

"Now, after you perform those tasks, if you don't get promoted you are working for the wrong company."

Great employees aren't born. They're molded, encouraged, nurtured and ... recognized.

CHAPTER

11

Rewrite the Policy Manual

OK, here's your first job as a manager:

Find every copy of every policy manual that your company has ever issued. Then insert an extra page in the front of the manual that reads: "Every employee of our company has the authority to do things outside this policy manual when the situation dictates."

I am not big on written policies. There should just be guidelines. You can't possibly write a policy that covers every situation.

Some employees love to say, "I wish I could help you but the policy says 'blah-blah-blah.'"

Give me a break.

I think most policy manuals are written to make the president feel good because he can refer to it, see it in writing, and quote himself.

Some policies are crazy to begin with. For example, some companies would rather have customers pay bills through the mail rather than bringing the bills to the office and paying them in person. Cricket, a provider of cell phone service, now charges $5 when a customer comes into the store to pay her monthly bill. Western Wireless from Seattle has a similar policy, charging customers $3 to pay their bills at the office. How dumb is that? When these companies start losing customers, they will blame the economy.

Policies can seem to make sense when written, but can become ridiculous in practice. For example, after the Columbine school shooting incident, many public schools decided to tighten up their security policies.

This was a sensible response to a perceived danger. What was not so sensible is how these new policies were sometimes carried out.

The policy went into effect in the Denver public school system, stating that anyone who brings a weapon to school, such as a knife or a gun, will be expelled from school. It was explained to the public as a "no tolerance rule," which is, in my opinion, just plain stupid. With a "no tolerance rule," no one has to think.

One day, while rushing to get ready for school, a ten-year-old girl accidentally picked up her mother's lunch instead of her own. Unfortunately for the little girl, her mother's lunch contained a paring knife, which was to be used to peel the apple that was also located inside the sack.

Noticing the contents, the little girl realized she had accidentally grabbed the wrong lunch – her mother's. Playing by the rules, the ten-year-old turned her lunch in to the principal. Instead of being thanked for following the rules, the little girl and her mother were shocked when the girl's positive behavior was not reinforced. The girl was immediately suspended!

The principal said that it was not his fault, explaining, "We have a zero-tolerance policy." How lacking in leadership.

A leader knows the rules and interprets each situation according to the facts.

Do you see what the principal taught that ten-year-old and her classmates?

It's obvious.

The lesson the school taught the little girl could be titled, "Lie the next time."

The principal did not have the courage to stand up for what was an innocent mistake. The ten-year-old was punished just as if she had been a criminal. How sad – and how lasting the impression.

A good manager understands the intent of the policies. If you train your managers to look for the intent of the rules, then employees will learn to understand how to interpret policy for individual situations. As with many other customer service lessons, this is one best demonstrated by the boss.

Give your front-line employees as much authority as possible

I always seem to get in situations that show how *not* to do things.

I went to a drugstore to return an item that hadn't ever been opened. The refund was $4.97.

The clerk at the register said she "could not do this." She had to call for a supervisor while I and four other people waited for the supervisor to OK the refund.

You would have thought I was robbing the store as four other people watched my face become increasingly red as I waited for this big refund.

But the policy at the drugstore was for only a supervisor to handle refunds, even such a simple one.

My suggestions for this company could save them a lot of money.

First, fire the clerk and save her salary expense. Second,

replace the fired clerk by putting the supervisor into the check stand. He still gets to wear his "supervisor" badge.

The only change is that he is now working in the check stand. According to the store, the supervisor is the only one who can approve a $4.97 refund.

Do you really need to have an employee who isn't empowered to take care of a simple customer request?

Forgiving late charges

Even when you do have policies, you can't count on your employees to follow them. That is why you have to appeal to employees' common sense and give them plenty of examples about the proper way to handle customers.

And in a company with 15,000 employees, managers have to understand the rationale of the policies as well as the rules.

For instance, we rent videotapes and we have late charges to control getting the tapes back.

However, sometimes a customer gets angry about the late charges for one reason or another.

I specifically told our employees, "Despite the policy, if the customer is obviously upset over the late charges, waive the late fee."

I want the customer to be happy when a videotape is returned. I would explain to the employees that they should be so appreciative when the tapes were returned that they should go around the service desk and hug the customer for returning the tape. Why? Because, when a customer has returned a tape, it can be rented again by someone else.

It can't be rented when it's at the customer's house, can it?

A customer sent a letter to me, telling me our store is "cheap." He had a late charge issue.

His children are like my children. They know how to go to the store to rent the tapes, they just don't know how to take them back.

His letter described his encounter with a head clerk named Jean.

He told Jean that his kids rented the tape "unbeknownst to him" and the tapes were around the house a number of days.

He asked Jean if she could help him with the late charges. Jean asked, "How much are the late charges?"

The customer said, "$10.00."

Jean started to negotiate, which was a mistake.

Jean asked, "How about $5.00?"

The customer paid the $5.00, but he was still mad.

So he wrote the president of the company (me) a letter to vent some of his anger.

I asked the store manager to handle it. The manager appeared at the customer's house the next day with the $5.00 he had paid for late charges, along with a $10.00 gift certificate as an apology for our "insensitivity" to his problem. If a customer is angry about late charges, don't negotiate a lower charge, just waive the charges. Then the customer goes away happy.

Let's dissect this situation.

The customer is wrong. The customer owed the late charges. But he's still the customer and now he is mad. He is worth at least $5,000 a year in purchases at one of our stores. By waiving the late charges, he's a happy customer and will continue to spend that $5,000. Seems like a better outcome to me than having him write an angry letter to the president. Remember – wrong customers spend money.

Another videotape incident illustrates the stick-to-the-policy-no-matter-what attitude.

A woman who had a problem at one of our stores called me. She had gone to the store two weeks prior and had rented two videotapes. The next day, a death occurred in her family; her family had to leave the state and her family was gone nine days.

When they got home, she went to the store to return the borrowed tapes and rent another one.

She approached the clerk on duty and explained what happened. The clerk wanted to charge her $18 for late charges.

She asked to see the manager and discovered, after an interminable wait at the counter, that the manager was off duty.

The clerk would not let her rent another tape until she paid the late charge. She negotiated the fee down to $10 and then was allowed to rent the other tape.

When she got home from the store and told her husband about her experience, he said, "There is no way that what you were told is actually the store's policy. Call the company president."

Of course she did. Now she was demanding to know the store's policy.

I replied, "First of all, you do not owe us any late charges."

"Oh yes, I owe you some late charges," she said.

"Not anymore, you don't. Please give me your

address. I must apologize. Obviously, we did a poor job of training our staff."

Silence – and then, "Oh no, it's not your fault."

When a customer starts feeling sorry for you, then you know the crisis is over. Always take the blame for an error. Even if you are right on the facts, the customer does not want to be proven wrong.

I said, "Yes, it is our fault. The reason it is our fault is that our clerk thinks what he did was right."

During the course of our conversation, the woman mentioned that her husband had tried to buy the movie "Harvey" with James Stewart, and he was disappointed that he could not find it. Before the call ended, I got her address. Then, I called the manager telling him to take back the $10 late charge, find the movie "Harvey" and deliver it to the customer free-of-charge.

"In addition," I said, "After you do that, I want you to ask the clerk why he did what he did. Do not chew him out or write him up. We want to learn about how he saw this situation."

The next day the customer called me, thrilled about how we had handled her complaint. I thanked her. The manager reported to me that he had talked with the employee about the situation, just as I had suggested.

According to the manager, in the employee's perception, "the customer didn't seem that mad and I was only trying to make money for the company."

I really did appreciate our employee trying to look out for the company interest. But we had to re-educate the employee to make him aware that the best thing he could do for our company was to give all customers the benefit of the doubt.

When a customer calls to complain

A policy must permeate all levels of a business in order for it to become a real policy. We established that even the switchboard operator has to appreciate how important it is when an irate customer calls.

Our telephone operators were directed that, in the case of a cranky caller, they were to locate someone to take care of the problem.

Immediately.

I told everyone, "If you receive a call from an unhappy customer and that caller was sent to or had requested the wrong department, don't transfer the call. Tell the customer you will get the right person to call you back."

The reason for this policy is that when a call is transferred, the person the customer wants may not be in… and it becomes a nightmarish merry-go-round. I get annoyed when I hear that an already cranky customer had to talk to four or five people before reaching the right person who was able to solve the problem.

The moral of this one is: give employees the latitude to use their judgment when the situation warrants. It requires training, training and more training. It also requires that all levels of management agree with this idea and use it in their dealings with customers.

But I think you'll find that when employees are encouraged to use their own sensible judgment and err on the side of the customer, the interactions with irate customers will be less frequent and result in more business for the company.

CHAPTER

12

Taking Care of Problems

Did you ever notice how unsolved problems have a tendency to grow bigger and bigger until they explode?

That is why I believe a well-run company has to have employees and managers who take care of problems as they arise.

Here.

Now.

On the spot.

I hate phone purgatory. You know the feeling you receive after you dial someone and you get the complicated messages that tell you what happens when you press buttons #1 through #10? The machine starts out by saying, "Your call is very important to us." If it were that important, a real, live, breathing person would answer the phone.

After button # 10, you can no longer remember what the voice mail said about who or what was where ... on and on and on, until the last button promises that you can talk with a live human.

However, you still are speaking to a machine. That's where the promise to be connected to a live human just came from – that's right – a machine.

Then, the machine starts again, this time with, "Due to a high volume of calls, we are unable to respond to your call right now. Please hold."

Isn't that fun?

Presidents of corporations ought to try calling themselves.

If that isn't enough, another phone irritant happens when a secretary answers, asking, "Who may I say is calling and what does this concern?"

I have always felt that who is calling is not a secretary's business.

Neither is why the caller is calling.

That's why I always made a special effort to answer my own phone when I was in the office. When I was out of the office, my secretaries knew to take down the caller's name and phone number promising the caller that I would return the call.

I always returned my phone messages as soon as I could. If the caller was an irate customer, the secretary knew to track me down so I could call back quickly.

Courting bad publicity

Here is an example of how *not* to take care of a problem:

I read recently in the local paper about a problem a local supermarket had. A lady was shopping in the store and as she lifted a six-pack of soda pop, the soda stack came tumbling down on her head. Fifteen cans hit her head, her knuckles, her eye and lip. There was lots of blood. The store manager attended to her with ice and an accident report. The manager asked her if she wanted to call the EMT. She said she would rather see her own physician.

She saw her doctor, and was black and blue and swollen for quite a while.

She gave the store a complete accident report, then waited for a return phone call. And waited. And waited.

Finally the store manager referred her to the risk management department. That wasn't exactly what she was expecting. I think she was hoping for an "I'm sorry" from the supermarket.

The writer of the newspaper article contacted a public relations person at the store, and he quickly got in the middle of it. The woman received a phone call from the risk management department, which assured her that the claim would be taken care of. The store sent her a $250 gift card, a fruit basket and flowers and a sincere apology. The public relations person told the newspaper reporter, "If I looked at this totally objectively, we should have followed up faster than we did."

This newspaper story is a perfect example of a manager not having the authority to take of this problem immediately – not five days later. That is why you don't send complaints to the office to be handled. The customer doesn't shop at your office. She shops at your store. And too many times a department or the legal experts say, "Don't do anything," because you might be admitting guilt and potential lawsuit. My response to that: I would rather risk a potential lawsuit in order to do the right thing. Doing what is right will probably not prevent a lawsuit, but if a lawsuit does occur, a company that shows compassion and concern about an accident will certainly look better than a company that ignores a bad situation.

There's the story of the elderly lady who sued McDonald's because she spilled very hot coffee on herself. All she wanted was for McDonald's to pay the doctor bill of $69. The claim went to the personnel department and they refused to pay it, saying it was her fault. Guess what. The customer won a huge settlement in court. McDonald's earned that payment.

Meeting customers on their home turf

Sometimes you get involved in a situation too late and have to play catch-up.

When I was a district manager, a woman wrote to the company president telling him that she was very unhappy with a particular incident and the way the store (under my supervision) managed the incident.

She even told my boss, "All of my neighbors are switching stores," due to the situation, especially because of the way the employees treated her.

I already knew that I had problems with this store.

Unfortunately, I had waited a little too long to start fixing the situation. My philosophy usually is to give the store manager a good chance to resolve things before I intervene.

From the look of this situation, it was time to make my move.

I called the irate customer and asked her if she could invite the other unhappy neighbors to her house. I promised her that if she did this, I would personally come to her house to discuss all of their concerns. She could not believe that had made this offer. She tested my promise by scheduling a meeting.

Five of the angry neighbors – all women – showed up for the meeting.

I arrived at her house, arms filled with free goods –

cake, ice cream and a large ham. For over an hour, I listened to the complaints. I shared inside information on how our stores work, and told the women how happy I was that they took the time to write to the president about their dissatisfaction.

I asked them to give me a chance to correct the issues and give us another chance to better our performance.

The next day, the formerly irate woman wrote another letter to the president, this time saying the following:

"You are truly to be congratulated for several reasons:

"First, for having an executive respond to my complaint letter so promptly and pleasantly. This neighborhood is a small, close-knit area where the word spreads quickly. We were surprised and pleased to receive a response from your company so promptly to my letter that shows you do care what your customers think about the store.

"Secondly, Mr. Gallegos must be a valued employee. He is an excellent representative – we had a very pleasant meeting.

"Mr. Gallegos listened to us, with tactful questions, drew out points of likes and dislikes, gave us good information on buying products and gave us insight into some of the problems management has in running a store.

"All of this Mr. Gallegos did with intelligence, charm and humor.

"It was an enjoyable and informative meeting.

"He turned us into loyal customers once again!

"Thank you for having Mr. Gallegos as your district manager."

Now, here is what she hand wrote at the bottom of the copy of the letter she sent to me:

"Dear Don,

"I had to laugh. The very next day I was in your store and I could already see the difference."

It is interesting to note that at the time of her visit I hadn't even been back to that store yet to make the changes. But she PERCEIVED it to be great because someone cared to give the customer attention when she needed it.

I will treasure that letter – always.

Special orders

One way that managers and employees can keep customers coming back to the store is to go out of the way to meet all the customers' needs.

Our company designed a special order program so that we would order anything a customer requested.

After all, even though we stocked about 48,000 items, we could not possibly stock everything or anticipate special requests. We would special order a product for a customer and store that product in a back room. To make things even more convenient for the customer, our policy allowed the customer to purchase one item from a case. The customer did not have to buy the entire case as part of a special order.

However, if the customer did choose to do this we would discount the case. We called this service "S.O.S." (SPECIAL ORDER SERVICE).

One day, a woman wanted Albertson's private label mayonnaise (one of our competitors), so our manager went to Albertson's supermarket and purchased a case of their mayonnaise. Then he called the woman, telling her that, from now on, when she wanted a jar of Albertson's private label mayonnaise she would be able to obtain it at his office.

He told her that all she had to do was to visit our store and ask the clerk to get the Albertson's mayonnaise for her.

"And," he added, "It's cheaper here."

When cashiers wear winter coats, it is time to remodel

When I first became district manager, I was assigned some of the stores in the worst physical condition in the whole chain.

The stores were good enough to carry on business as usual, but they were getting a bit frayed around the edges. One such store was scheduled for remodeling in approximately six months following my promotion to district manager.

One cold, wintry day, I visited this store. I was surprised to see that the people who were checking customers were dressed warmer than I was and they were inside the store!

The checkers were checking with gloves on, scarves around their necks and their teeth chattering. It was interesting to watch the checkers make change with gloved fingers and to watch customers receiving change, also with gloves on – coins dropping in every direction.

I could not believe the conditions under which our employees were working. I asked one of the checkers to tell me how long this had been going on. She told me that she had been there for nine years and that these conditions had been the same all that time.

This store was 27 years old and probably had seen four or five different district managers and a host of different store managers during that time. In all that time and through the long lineage of managers, NO ONE had even attempted to alleviate this problem.

I asked the manager of this store, "Why can't we do something?"

He told me that he had tried for at least five years and the answer he always received was, "Don't worry, we will fix it during the remodeling of the store, in the middle of the summer."

Summer would come and go – for years – with no improvement.

The reason this area of the store was so cold was that there were two entrances located at opposite ends of the store; one on the north side and the other on the south side. When the doors opened, the wind would blow across the front-end lobby, just where the check-out stands were located.

Of course, the checkers were caught right in the middle of the wind tunnel. I asked my boss, the director of operations, if we could do something about this situation. I felt confident that he would see the answer that I saw but I wanted him to state the remedy before I did.

He said, "We should wait until we do the remodeling." He shrugged his shoulders, "It's been like that for twenty-seven years."

There was a moment of silence before I said, "Yes, I understand, but do we have to make it twenty-eight?"

I consulted the construction manager to see if we could do something now. He said, "Yes, we could put up a temporary vestibule which would shield the wind from going inside the store."

However, in order to accomplish this he would need a capital expenditure request signed by both my boss and me. I realized from our conversation that my boss was not going to approve it. I knew I had to see the president of the company. After explaining the problem to the president from my viewpoint, we got the OK.

I had gone over my boss' head – several steps up the "food chain" of the line of authority in the company –- and he was angry.

That anger was short-lived. My boss saw the result of my efforts accompanied by the undying gratitude of the newly thawed employees who credited him with fixing the problem.

I admit it. I did not follow procedure. I did go over my boss' head because I figured out that the comfort of the employees and customers would far outweigh my boss' initial displeasure.

After the installation, you would have thought I had given those checkers a huge raise. They were so pleased with the "upgrade in conditions" that they retired their wooly gloves and earmuffs like football players retiring their winning jerseys.

Happiness did not end there.

Customers wrote letters to the president, congratulating him on "finally doing something for our people." In response to all this glowing appreciation, the president thanked my boss for having had the foresight to "get this done."

Were my actions risky? You bet they were. However, it was the right thing to do. It is interesting to note that, "up the food chain," people were sitting in a warm office saying that checkers didn't need the store heat fixed. The working conditions had remained uncomfortable over a long period of time. Management got away with having lowered the bar and the employees put up with the discomfort.

One more thing – the best consequence of the actions happened – productivity rose as quickly as the heat in the store.

Accounting for changes

Many times I have been asked about the cost and the rate of return on some of the things we do. You know, you can cost your way out of business by trying to account for everything you do. Obviously, you have to control costs. But in my experience, when things get tough, the first thing we tend to do is cut costs that affect the customer. That is a big mistake.

Accountants love to take on cost analysis in every task and show that the numbers don't make sense. But you can't justify by the cost of doing something without looking at the big picture. I remember when accounting wanted to show the cost of our "no questions asked refund policy." They asked me if I wanted to see it.

I said no.

I know what our top line is – sales, and what our bottom line is – profit. Everything in between is how we get there.

Never let accounting dictate your marketing

practices. I remember accountants telling me the cost of our free cookie program was $300,000 a year. It would be easy to stop, but how do you put a price tag on the happiness of children (and their parents) and the extra shopping trips that result because of our cookie policy?

Accountants can run you out of business in their uncontrolled zeal to save money.

CHAPTER

13

Summing Up

I hope by this time you are convinced that Americans have lowered the bar too much on customer service. I hope you will go out today and insist that everyone in your business treat customers with respect. Whenever there is a question or dispute, give your customers the benefit of the doubt.

And when you are a customer, when you're buying a product or service, you have to demand that businesses treat you properly. If everyone insists on being treated appropriately, we will be starting a movement to make sure superior customer service becomes the norm and not the rare exception.

I have one final thought. Too many people get caught up in the routine and bureaucracy of everyday life to really appreciate all that life has to offer.

I have always believed in trying to make every day count. Many people do not try to make a difference in someone's life every day. They are always focused on the future.

In our youth, we count the days until we are 18 and are "of age." Then, the count is on until we reach 21, which is "legal age." Then we count down until we are married and start our family.

After a couple has been married for a while, they count the days until they have children. Then, after three kidlets, the wife says repeatedly, "If we could just get these kids in school, then life would be perfect, we'll be happy." The husband agrees.

The kids start school and those years begin to fly by. Then the wife says, "If we could just get these kids through high school, then life will be better and we'll be happy." The husband agrees. Suddenly, those years are gone and have become memories.

After all the children are out of high school, the man and his wife are a little older and whatever hair he has left has turned gray and is much thinner.

Then the wife says, "My goodness, now if we can just get them through college, life will be better and we'll be happy."

Then the day of graduation arrives for each of their kids...

The man says to his wife, "Now that the kids are out of college, I think I can retire at age 60." The wife says, "Great, I'll count the days with you. Then we'll be happy."

He reaches age 60 and says to his wife, "We haven't enough money; you'll have to wait until I'm 65." His wife again responds, "I'll count the days with you and then we'll be happy."

At age 65, he retires and gets his gold watch.

They fly to Hawaii and there they are – sitting on the beach. He turns to his wife and says, "Well, we finally made it." She says, "So?"

What do you think happened? They missed the trip...

Some day, you are going to be 65. You might as well enjoy the trip along the way.

I would hate to read an article in the newspaper saying, "Don Gallegos just announced his retirement at age 65 and now he is going to do what he always wanted to do."

65 years? What a waste!

One evening, I woke up in the middle of the night with this thought:

"LIFE IS SHORT. YOU'RE DEAD FOR A LONG TIME."

A final thought

From all the years I have spent in management guiding customer service policy to what I am involved in now, which is consulting and speaking, I know that the customer service journey never ends. No matter what is going on in the world, we should never stop asking the right questions regarding human behavior and attitude.

Do we like the people with whom we work? Do we need to like those people in order to provide good service and attention to others? Do we take time to be polite to one another? Do we help others when they need help? Do we need to be invited to help others or do we take the risk to help first and ask questions later – act and then ask?

My wife tells me that I "attract bad service." Perhaps that's a true statement because I spend so much time searching for "good service." I keep looking for a step beyond the average standard.

As a nation, we seem to be lowering the bar instead of raising expectations set by example.

I seek from others what I think we, as a public,

deserve. It is how I serve others. It is how I wish to be served.

I believe that customer service, at any given time, is a demonstration of the public's attitudes regarding humanity.

May your personal customer service journey be filled with adventure, happiness and great understanding and fulfillment.

Pass it on and don't miss the trip.